People's Prison

People's Prison

★ ★ ★

GEOFFREY JACKSON

READERS UNION
Group of Book Clubs
Newton Abbot 1974

CONTENTS

CONTENTS

PART FIVE: THE RETURN

ILLUSTRATIONS

Photographs 2, 3, 4, 5, 6, 7, 8 and 9 reproduced by courtesy of Associated Press; 1 reproduced by courtesy of *Woman and Home*; photograph 10 by courtesy of Press Association.

To my wife, and our son

FOREWORD

My Uruguayan kidnappers, known as the Movimiento de Liberación Nacional, had adopted their alternative designation of 'Tupamaros' from another century and another corner of Latin America. Túpac-Amaru was the last scion of the Incas, brought up in eighteenth-century Peru as a Spanish hidalgo. Outraged by the oppression of his fellow Indians – by Spanish settlers conceivably no more authoritarian than his own ancestors – he launched a belated movement for indigenous rights.

Inevitably it failed; and in 1784 Túpac-Amaru was executed in Lima, torn apart by four cart-horses. His name, in the more Spanish-sounding abbreviation of Tupamaro, became a synonym for 'trouble-maker' throughout the scattered Spanish settlements of eighteenth-century Latin America. Almost two centuries later that term of opprobrium was adopted by a small group of Uruguayan urban guerrillas, dedicated to the overthrow of the present order of society, as a badge of honour.

Under its emblem the Tupamaros found it legitimate and worth their while, for most of a year, to deprive my country of its ambassador's universally recognized immunities, and my person – and family – of an equally universal basic human right. They also, in due course, found it expedient, or right, to return me to life, and my life to me, after all.

Jagdhaus Lienbach, Austria   GEOFFREY JACKSON

PART ONE

PREMONITION AND CAPTURE

Chapter 1

M Y epic, melodrama, misadventure, or whatever label it merits, began officially on 8th January 1971. To me it has always seemed instead a simple long haul, and to have begun perhaps as much as a year before its ostensible starting-date. Could we but consult them, I have no doubt that for its authors too the beginnings of their operation dated far back into 1970.

That was when I – and even more so the intuitions of my wife – began to sense that the malaise of Uruguay was coming too pointedly into focus over our own heads, and to interfere too directly in the happiness of our own lives. For an official, even more so for a diplomat overseas, obsessiveness is an occupational hazard which he drills himself to avoid; a hypothesis too strenuously deployed can all too easily assume the aspect of an hallucination. But it was quite early in 1970 when I began to sense that accumulation of recurrently anomalous situations which the late Ian Fleming defined so neatly. His James Bond says somewhere that 'Once is happenstance, twice is coincidence, and three times is enemy action.' When, after a relatively quiet life, nocturnal telephone-calls begin to proliferate; when one's hitherto pleasantly solitary walks along beaches and sand-dunes and in pine-forests begin to bristle with horizon-marching silhouettes and sudden encounters with the courting young in unlikely trio formation; when one's golf-game – and not only one's own – begins regularly to be intercepted by casual youthful spectators on remote fairways; when for the third time one's path is crossed by professional violence literally on one's own doorstep – by this time the least perceptive of mortals begins to grasp that, however much the world around him may be changing, his own private world is changing still more.

This subtle change of mood coincided, in our case, with

infinitely more sinister symptoms, internally and, especially, internationally. Internally there was an intensification of urban guerrilla activism in the Uruguayan capital which both swamped the conventional security forces – the police – and also confronted the armed forces with a challenge for which neither their nor the Uruguayan nation's tradition of military abstention from internal and political affairs had prepared them. Externally the march south of diplomatic kidnapping, and worse, had taken a major and disastrous turn, with the abduction and subsequent murder of Count von Spreti, the German Ambassador to Guatemala, early in 1970. Similar instances accumulated and grew closer – the successive kidnappings in Brazil of the United States, German and Swiss Ambassadors, with a mounting successive toll of hostages demanded in exchange for, happily, the release intact of the ambassadors in question. Aberrant but closer demonstrations of violence also occurred – a narrow escape by a young American Consul in Porto Alegre, in Southern Brazil not far from the Uruguayan border, and the daylight hold-up of the Swiss Embassy offices in Montevideo, after which the Swiss Ambassador carried on as usual, with characteristic national phlegm, despite a harrowing personal experience which, till the invaders left his premises, bore every sign of an intended kidnap.

It seemed to me that telegrams and dispatches were no longer enough. This was one of those intangible situations in which the cobweb touch of impending violence was too subtle to convey other than in person. Fortunately a conference in London of Commercial Officers from Latin America was pending, and nowadays all ambassadors recognize themselves as Commercial Officers – myself not least, both by training and inclination. So I decided to go to England myself, and seize the opportunity to make it clear to those concerned that, however hypothetical, a situation existed which at any moment might transform itself into a possibly brutal reality.

Revealing of the atmosphere is that, though the conference in question was a brief men-only affair, it never occurred either to my wife or to myself that she should be left behind. My ambassadorial first-class ticket 'on the firm' was balanced rather ludicrously by an economy-class ticket for her on me. Our aloofness to class barriers, however mystifying to the stewardess, meant at least that we had the comfort of each other's company rather than an increasingly uncertain separation with the Atlantic and Equator between us.

At home I met with a sympathetic and understanding awareness of the situation in Latin America generally, and in my part of it in particular. This was all that I needed. It was sufficient that I should leave behind an account which was not seen as imaginative or overstated, and which left my Department unlikely to be taken by surprise when what was growing increasingly ominous might materialize. Typical of those moments when the weight of nightmare, if not moved from my shoulders, was at least shifted to a position of relative tolerability, was a laconic encounter with one of our most senior officials.

He hoped that things were not too unbearable, on which the analogy occurred to me to ask him if he had ever had mice. I needed to say no more; he shook his head sympathetically. In the next few weeks I was to know all too well, as was my wife, that sensation which needs no explanation to those who have endured the presence of mice, or rats, behind the woodwork, that certainty of an intelligence and strength always invisible, but always there, present, vigilant, somehow malignant.

My son, though we spoke little of these things, was only too conscious of my concern. In consequence, on my return to my post, he wrote to me a quite memorable letter which, indeed, may later have affected my whole life and survival. He did not disguise his anxiety that I refused to withdraw myself from risks which he considered were no longer for my generation. He understood well, however, why I could not fob these off onto someone else, and had no doubts as to my capacity to support whatever I might have to confront. This letter was to remain in the forefront of my mind for an important part of the near future.

It was with a sad heart therefore that I, and in particular I have no doubt his brave mother, took the aircraft back to Montevideo. We felt better when our landfall from Freetown in Sierra Leone, across the Atlantic, brought us straight up the River Plate, from which we looked down on a sunlit and idyllic Montevideo, with our own roof and garden clearly visible in tiny detail some thirty thousand feet below.

Chapter 2

WE were not to guess that this satellite vision of almost extraterrestrial placidity and beauty was instead a façade for events, taking place at that moment, of a swift and implacable violence only to be surpassed by the brutality and tragedy of their outcome. Our transatlantic aircraft landed in Buenos Aires barely in time for us to be hustled across the apron onto the connecting plane over to Montevideo. There, as we emerged to greet Carrasco Airport, the welcoming faces were not this time smiling; their anxious expressions were justified by the tenseness of unprecedented numbers of security forces, by a noisy motor-cycle escort back to the pretty suburb of Pocitos, site of the Embassy residence, and by the tale my Deputy had to tell.

That morning a terrorist commando had kidnapped a young Second Secretary of the United States Embassy, another diplomatic officer having managed to escape the attention of his would-be captors. Another commando had intercepted and kidnapped a United States police official, Mr. Dan Mitrione, attached to the Uruguayan Government on a technical-aid training basis. The young diplomat had escaped by a remarkable feat of gymnastics: though wrapped up like a side of bacon he had contrived to perform a back-flip over the tail-gate of the flat truck in which he was being transported. He was picked up, unhurt either by his fall or by the following traffic, and I can only attribute his escape to his youth and fitness, together with the incentive, above and beyond his normal evident intrepidity, of just having become the father of twins. The fact remains that never again did the Tupamaros use a flat truck for an abduction; after the escape of Gordon Jones, closed vans were *de rigueur*. As for the late Mr. Mitrione,

Latin American history will always record how, a week or so later, he was found murdered in circumstances which I believe left a large proportion of his Tupamaro 'executioners' themselves with a heavy conscience and with misgivings for the future.

From this moment on I too was to have a heavy heart and little peace of mind. The increasing recourse of the Tupamaros to abduction needed to be considered seriously in the light of its use against diplomats by similarly orientated guerrilla bodies in neighbouring Brazil. Already, for greater or lesser periods of time, important Uruguayan figures had been captured and imprisoned – a banker of Italian origin, ransomed by friends, the Chairman of the National Energy Corporation, released, only to be recaptured after myself and held prisoner again, this time for more than a year. Shortly afterwards the Brazilian First Secretary was kidnapped, and then Dr. Claude Fly, an elderly, studious and frail soil-technician, whose capture and prolonged imprisonment have never made any sense. He was evidently of a most endearing disposition, even to his captors, and the legend of his courage persisting among my own custodians represented a source of inspiration and strength to me for which I shall always be grateful; when a man can be described by a Marxist- Leninist gaoler as 'a saint', then further canonization scarcely seems necessary.

The growing abundance of precedent was compounded daily by the intensified whiff of invigilation, by that ever stronger sense of the presence behind the arras, of movement and activity behind the wainscot. Life's anomalies multiplied preternaturally. Even the Montevideo traffic, which in its normal pattern has been compared by cynics to the lead-in to any Tupamaro hijacking, tended daily to yet further eccentricity, even on that ample criterion of tolerance. Barely a day passed without some car boring in on us at speed, I can only assume to test our responses. I noticed that, instead of the by now habitually encroaching light pick-up with its invariable two boys and a girl, increasingly heavy vehicles seemed to gravitate towards my large and powerful Daimler limousine. Such was the implacability of one such approach that, slowly and painstakingly, a wing was ripped off, in retrospect so dry a run for the almost identical circumstances of my capture as to be unmistakable.

The sense of being spied upon intensified and became at last regularly identifiable. At times I felt that my watchers, pursuers, scrutineers, had lost all sense of clandestinity, even of discretion. It became quite normal for myself, and for those members of my staff concerned, to recognize the same motor-scooter, with the same number-plate though perhaps a change of crew, skirmishing round the vicinity of the residence, then showing up as my official car was parking by the chancery offices. I remember one day drawing the attention of my 'retinue' to a young couple canood-ling by the steps leading into the office. They were leaning against each other, propped up by their motorized bicycle, arms round each other's waist, and with the young man singing – as for some reason I vividly recall – the Spanish version of 'I've got you under my skin'. I drew Mick's attention – more of Mick anon, for he was usually several jumps ahead of me in perceptivity – to them as undoubtedly a reconnaissance team. He agreed, but asked for my reasons, which were based on the fact that their expression did not correspond to their activity, and that their eyes had an opaque, obsidian quality, familiar from the 1948 'Bogotazo' and from many a Central American *coup*, instead of the spaniel-like languidity and luminosity normally associated with their age and ostensible state of mind. Mick however had recognized them by their number-plate, which he had earlier traced back to a university student of known terrorist affiliations.

Across the street from my home is a pretty if these days rather weather-beaten park, where on warm days and before or after football matches the people tend to gather, to rest and even to picnic. Suddenly however the hitherto occasional picnic seemed to convert itself into a nonstop rotating phenomenon. At virtually all times, in daylight at least, there was invariably a young family camped on the grass opposite, enjoying the warm weather which, in Montevideo, coincides exactly with the months leading up to and following my abduction. They were very normal people; the young husband would doze, and play with the baby; the young wife would play her transistor-radio and set out the picnic. But they were too recurrent, and their pattern of activity too identical, even though their apparent normality was such that I could not possibly denounce them – save to the highly experienced Mick – much less ask that they be sent away.

I do not however like to seem to be taken in, at any rate to myself and to those doing the taking, though the onlooker's opinion leaves me cold as a rule. I therefore left my invigilators in no doubt that they had been recognized, looking them straight in the eye as they passed me by. In consequence I believe that I was able to recognize some of them later, when I had only their eye to go by. One of the 'young mothers' was thus easily recognizable later, by, also, her tiny stature and full narrow mouth which, with her unmistakably Near Eastern eyes, were to make me wonder whether she – and a certain young interrogator who might well have been her brother – were not of East Mediterranean origin.

Further opportunities to look into the eye of the urban guerrillas crescendoed as the pace of their patrolling was accentuated, the size of the patrol vehicles seeming to increase in ratio to the intensity of their activity. A couple of days before my capture an opulent if elderly Buick sedan drove intermittently by my home for most of a day, while only the very day before a much-finned De Soto – a long extinct breed – crossed our bows on my way home from work. The face that looked out of the first was the face I saw in the mirror of my office Daimler when it drove me away on the first stage of my journey into captivity, while the long clown's face that loomed at me from the second was to appear later, rendered innocent by sleep, in an underground cage – one of the few Tupamaro faces disclosed to me by accident.

Chapter 3

IT may well seem, but must not for a moment be imagined, that we were all taking this situation with the passivity of a rabbit hypnotized – if so they be – by a snake. For one thing, there is an element of real indignity when, as more than once happened – on the way home from a meeting at the British School, or returning from some other nocturnal official function – a car pulls out into the side-street behind one, keeps its distance for several miles then, unpredictably, just turns away. My wife for one was all too conscious of such situations and, though how much I did not till long after know, almost frantically so at any delay or uncertainty in my own movements.

As long too as Mick was with me I knew that my safety was guarded, above and beyond the call of what in fact is normally a purely routine inspection duty. An intelligent and imaginative man is however almost invariably afflicted with the conscience and sense of duty which produce the volunteer and the willing overtime from among the ranks of the clock-watchers. In a way therefore I was relieved for him when he left on reluctant transfer. He had elaborated his own intelligence network far beyond the resources of his local contacts; they were able to do nothing about what he was able to convey to them.

So, I increasingly felt, if what was happening to me was personally intended, rather than just part of some vast, impersonal data-collecting training-task, then Mick's life was in real danger. I have little doubt that he would have been the first target had he been present at my eventual kidnapping, and so was thankful to know he was safe with his wife and family, particularly when, at last, I was safe again myself.

For these reasons I used the discretion I had always had, renewed after a special visit from home prompted by the August

kidnappings and the Mitrione killing, to forbid the use of fire-
arms by the bodyguard and back-up car I was now authorized to
employ. Their purpose was to provide an element of obstructive,
or even elusive, security only, and many was the time when Hugo,
my driver, would shrug the great hindquarters of my seven-
seater official Daimler at some suspiciously intrusive small
'camioneta', flicking it aside while signalling the fast little station-
wagon behind us to overtake and cut in briskly where the inter-
loper had wished to precede it.

Likewise we experimented with all the by now familiar
procedures of playing permutations on timing and routing to,
and especially back from, my office. I had always believed that I
was most exposed out of the centre of Montevideo, owing to the
narrow streets of the old down-town business centre, its complicated super-imposals on a basic gridiron street pattern, and the
pronounced individualism and unpredictability of its drivers at
which I have hinted already. Such a setting seemed to favour
neither attack nor getaway. Between the down-town and my
home lay the Rambla – to translate it as the Corniche rather than
the Prom would be to show a proper concern for Montevideo's
civic pride – a beautiful drive, but disconcertingly lonely and
deserted outside the rush-hours of morning, noon and evening.
So any added security derived from permutation was negated by
the exposure derived from abnormal solitude. Down-town we
had tried especially one alternative approach, via the docks; but
in the present depleted state of Uruguay's trade their desolation
and convolution seemed a positive incitement to kidnapping. So
only in the down-town did I feel safe, heaving a sigh of relief
each morning as I reached its crowded seclusion, and feeling
restive when I left it for the Rambla and, particularly, the network of thinly travelled roads and avenues through the parks
which were the only approach to my home. It was there, and
then, I believed my danger to lie.

Later I was to hear that it was our emphasis on caution in these
more exposed positions which had forced my captors to seek me
out in circumstances compelling them to an operation far more

elaborate, expensive and potentially costly to them than they had ever intended. They were acknowledgedly left with only one further stage of risk, which would have been my capture from an official function, in all probability with, or at any rate in the presence of, my wife.

Meanwhile work, and my official life, had to continue, as best as they could, despite the increasing sense of imprisonment in our own home. Ostensibly a British ambassador was no more exposed than any other, and a good deal less than some, one of whom, from a neighbouring country, remained effectively housebound after an ugly incident or two, running his chancery from his heavily guarded residence. He, by his geographical and political significance in Uruguay, was self-evidently a prime target for urban guerrilla attack. But conventional local opinion was that a British ambassador, with the affection of the whole Uruguayan nation behind him, would never be touched, let alone harmed, even by an Uruguayan insurgent. Britain's role in the independence of Uruguay, rising two centuries ago, remains fresh in its people's mind; but the question always in my mind was whether the philosophy, the ideology, of the Tupamaros allowed them to share that time-honoured interpretation.

It was not though for me to demonstrate my misgivings, in public, on official occasions, even within the diplomatic corps, on the discretion of some of whom – perhaps even on their benevolence and affiliations – I had my reservations, later to be justified by the frankness of my captors. To my staff, to the Uruguayan authorities, I could speak very bluntly; with them I could only accept that if this was normality it was normality of a totally new dimension. I realized that my by now hair-trigger vigilance must seem obsessive; yet in fairness to myself, when one visitor begged me not to see a Tupamaro behind every tree, it was barely a day or so later that they emerged in force to wrench me away from my accustomed reality.

In fairness too however to the author of such ill-timed solace, I accept that by this time I must have been becoming a trial to my family and to my friends. Virtual imprisonment in my admittedly large and beautiful garden, the forced abandonment of my favourite sea-shore and woodland walks, what P. G. Wodehouse's Bertie Wooster calls a sense of impending doom: all these encroachments oppressed me. By now I was bad company, and knew it – not least, I was to reproach myself, to my poor patient wife.

Chapter 4

I did not however know that, when I said goodbye to my wife rather more hastily than usual on the morning of 8th January 1971, it would often seem in retrospect to have been a very final goodbye and that, as far as 'au revoirs' go, it would have to suffice me for the greater part of a year.

I had an appointment with a British businessman in my office for 10.15 a.m., and I remember calling to my wife that, if I waited for her to finish her bath, I would keep him waiting; I have always insisted that no caller at a British Embassy should be kept waiting, least of all the travelling British businessman, that least acknowledged hero of our time. So I dashed into our bathroom and kissed her – I remember that her lips were wet – and told her that I would have the office ring her when I left to come home for lunch.

It was a beautiful morning, and the way we took to the Rambla was very quiet; the President had just left on a seaside holiday, taking with him many of the usual security forces. As always, I was relieved when we turned in from the open corniche into the narrow and crowded side-streets leading to my office, and I was joking with my driver as we edged slowly along the single lane left by the vehicles parked on either side. We were at a point where virtually every day we had to wait for delivery-trucks to finish unloading at one or other of the wayside stores, so I did not pay especial attention to a large red van – certainly of three, possibly of five tons – until it edged out from the kerb as we drew level. There was little room for my driver to swerve, but ample time for the truck-driver to realize and correct his mistake. I knew however that frequently they did not do so till after impact, and was not really surprised when, despite my driver's signals, he bored relentlessly into our left front wing. With a philosophical shrug, and obvious resignation to a coachwork job and some ineffectual insurance activity, Hugo opened his door to climb out and take particulars.

Instead, as the cab-door opened and the truck-driver leapt down, a young man stepped from nowhere and struck Hugo savagely over the head. Simultaneously there was a violent rattle of automatic weapons which continued for what to me seemed an endless time; one of its main constituents originated from a sub-machinegun concealed in a basket of fruit carried by an apparently innocuous bystander – my captors were very proud of this refinement, of which I was told repeatedly afterwards.

The driver of the truck climbed into my chauffeur's seat, and opened the opposite door for a second young man. A third put his arm round the door-pillar and expertly unlocked the back door from the inside, while a fourth, stationed next to me by the right-hand rear door, as Gilbert's young lawyer danced a dance like a semi-despondent fury, making frantic and furious signals at me, presumably to encourage me to open the door for him. This was done for him by the third young man, who had meanwhile climbed into the rear compartment by the now open door, on which Operative Number Four came in shooting – quite inexplicably, if my capture was the aim, because he nearly killed me, to quote him as he sat across my knee with his smoking automatic after two holes, in apparent slow motion, had appeared in the seat next to my leg and in the roof above my head. 'Almost I killed you, Old Man,' he yelled accusingly as he proceeded to hammer away at my head; nor had I any illusion that the epithet was chronologically slanted rather than affectionately intended, English-style.

I meanwhile was striving to spare my glasses which, almost instinctively, I decided I was going to need. It was perhaps foolish of me to reach into my inside pocket, though when my hand came out with my glasses-case the purity of my motives should have been evident enough to discourage Operative Number Three from, quite needlessly, struggling with and manhandling me, and Operative Number Four from administering first a classic pistol-whipping with the front end and gun-sight of his pistol, and then a brisk pounding from the butt end along my mastoid processes; it was to be many weeks before I was to see, much less feel, the last vestiges of this treatment.

By this time the car was beginning to move. With the same curious but I suppose perfectly normal sense of slow motion, helped out by one young man seeking to immobilize me while, for the first time in long years, someone aged more than a couple of years was sitting on my knee, I somehow had the leisure to study what was happening and who was executing it. My attackers were not masked – the last human faces I was to see for a long time. They were thoroughly conversant with the idiosyncrasies of the Daimler – its gear-shift, with some rather exotic characteristics for Montevideo; the door-locks; and the power-steering; I found my mind formulating the many circumstances in which this familiarity could have been acquired.

Two of the team gave me the impression of having so full a mouthful of teeth as to have some too many, till I realized that this appearance was an expression, a rictus, a grimace of sheer tension; the other two were perfectly composed. The youngster badgering me with his pistol – for which I was afterwards told he was disciplined – was very young, little more than a sixth-form schoolboy, and so over-excited that I wondered if he was not drugged. He was butter-blond, with a wide mouth displaying rather slab-like teeth and too much gum, while his companion, perhaps a little older, was a handsome boy with waving light-brown hair and the large and luminous eyes – in his case hazel – which as the months passed and eyes and hoods were all I knew, I realized are rather characteristic of the Uruguayan young. Both were shorter than I – and I am not tall – but stocky and heavily muscled, and with blindingly swift muscular reflexes.

Our driver, whom I could see clearly in the mirror, was, as I have said, a face I had met recently. He had blunt features, a moustache half-way Zapata-style and, again, this rictus of tension, concentration or – I would not blame them – sheer fright. Three of the four I would recognize again instantly, were I to live to be a centenarian.

I was also striving desperately to see through the driver's mirror what might be happening behind me, to my chauffeur prone on the pavement, and to Walter and Carlos whom I had briefly been able to see springing out of my back-up car into what at any rate sounded like a hail of machinegun fire. I prayed that my assailants would have recognized in time that they were unarmed, and that if I myself emerged unscathed in the next minutes I should soon have reassurance about them.

But I was not to enjoy for long the privilege of literal hindsight or, for that matter, of any kind of continued vision. My less aggressive attacker was by now struggling to bandage my eyes with a blindfold that was far too small; their otherwise painstaking reconnoitring had not disclosed to them the fact that I take a seven-and-five-eighths in hats. His more violent partner would hit me with his pistol and then, because not unnaturally I suppose I blinked, he would hit me again and yell to me to close my eyes; very quickly I reached the stage of 'in for a penny in for a pound', and did all the peeping I could.

Our departure continued as spectacular as its beginning. The collision-truck had ripped the left-hand front wing so that it was flapping loose against the wheel, making a much amplified version of the noise achieved by small boys who fix a strip of cardboard into their bicycle spokes. I was hoping that this tremendous racket, plus the congestion normal to the vicinity, would attract immediate retaliation, and hopefully rescue, by some passing patrol. But I suddenly remembered that, coming in from the Rambla, even the usual sentry-post overlooking its length from the top of the gasworks had been absent. My heart sank, as I realized that the President, having left town, must have taken much of the available trained and equipped personnel with him. From the unnatural emptiness of the down-town streets it was also evident that an elaborate and effective road-blocking system had been deployed to free my captors' egress into the suburban road-system, by ten a.m. already in a state of post-rush-hour unencumberment.

Our Tupamaro driver was further clenching his teeth and

stretching his lips into a flat oblong as he wrestled with the still perhaps not wholly familiar steering of the Daimler, its un-familiarity compounded by the noise and friction from the torn coachwork. But he kept up a fair speed, and within five minutes we stopped in a long and, to my disappointment, very empty street which I recognized. It ran along the side of a convent, and at the end of it I could see the river, which at Montevideo is effectively the ocean itself. I looked at it with longing as I initiated the first part of a contingency-plan I had long contemplated for such an eventuality. As my captors hustled me out, towards an elderly and amateurishly blue-painted Chevrolet van, I swooned. It was not difficult; my head was already dizzy from the knocks it had taken. Yet all things considered I was in remarkably good shape – good enough to make a break for it had there been the least cover. But there was not. Bleak, rather grey, and empty, the street stretched away like some drawing-book demonstration of perspective. At least, I thought, my captors can have the effort of carrying me to the next stage in my transportation. Just as they were hoisting me into the open doors of the waiting van, I suddenly heard from behind me the anxiously piping voice of, evidently, some nice little old lady, who wished to know if she could help with the poor gentleman. No, replied one of my captors; he was in good hands, having been taken sick and being moved to hospital. I decided that to exploit the cover offered by one nice old lady would do her no good, and me still less, and heard the van-doors slam to with resignation.

Even so, and so soon as this, I was already able to inject some relative relief into my resignation. I started on what was to be a long, continuous and constantly updated process of inward accountancy. On the credit side I congratulated myself that my wife could count at any rate on a widow's pension, and that my son was in every sense a grown man, and self-supporting. My briefcase contained nothing that could injure or embarrass my government, or for that matter add to my own danger – a distinction, it occurred to me, worthy of inclusion in a method-ology of instructions drawn up when, so short a time ago, wayside kidnapping, and situations of 'parallel power', were not a consideration in ambassadorial security. My work was up to date, and my annual report for 1971 already sent to type. My wife and I were agreed on what she was to do, and my government already knew my views for such a contingency which she would, on her return, re-emphasize for surety after the event; I could count on her for that, come what may. Through the quite extraordinary calm which had come over me I felt the first stirring of the profound grief, and of regret for time wasted offset against gratitude for many blessings, which were to occupy my thoughts in so many long hours of long days and months to come.

But more urgent thoughts took priority. My more violent companion ripped up my right-hand jacket-sleeve, then my shirt-sleeve. I watched with dispassionate amazement as my much-loved gold-and-silver Mexican cuff-links – the gift of a dear Honduran friend now dead – held firm while a double cuff of sea-island cotton, with four well-stitched buttonholes, ripped through like tissue paper under one vicious pull. I was never to see my Aztec cuff-links again after that first day, though the shirt is with me still, reminding me how for so long it served as garment, bed-linen, towel, pyjama, light-screen, handkerchief and, at last, as a good honest shirt again. It also serves as a salutary reminder, when with the passing of time I find myself forgetting the strictly violent aspects of my captivity in favour of its more contemplative or even argumentative moments. It is as well always to keep in mind that behind all the ideological protestations of the New Revolution lies the ultimate and unchanging sanction of raw force. There are those whose tangible reminder is less humdrum and innocuous than a ripped shirt-cuff, and also those remembered but no longer available to be reminded by some such cherished *trivia*.

The purpose of this operation was evidently to get at an artery, either to inject, or to extract or – as proved to be the case – both. One of my captors had been feverishly attempting to jab a needle into the back of my left hand, but gave it up and ordered the van and its bouncing to be stopped. Though all too conscious of the ominous overtones which I have just recalled, I asked him if he was trying to tattoo the back of my hand with the Tupamaro emblem and, for the first time, I heard a Tupamaro laugh. But when he had drawn his blood-sample and administered his first of many drugs, the joke was over, he and his friends demonstrated, as I made my first acquaintance with the infamous do-it-yourself handcuff of the urban guerrilla. I was to wear it again a couple of times, and can only assume that this butterfly of heavy steel wire, with its two-way ratchet in the middle, is a standard underground appliance, made up from one or another of the textbooks of revolution which proliferate in the paperback market available to students, school-children and other young-folk-in-a-hurry today.

This seemed an appropriate moment to deploy a not very convincing method of seeking to attenuate some of these painful procedures, by mentioning the fact that I had some heart trouble many years ago, as a young ambassador of forty-four in the Republic of Honduras. There was not time to explain, nor would my immediate captors have been interested to know, that it had never been clear if that incident had been an authentic infarct or some simple collapse after paratyphoid and an overdose of antibiotics. In any case the response of my blond gadfly was, as I might have expected from his Punch-and-Judy syndrome, to say 'Quiet!' and rap me over the head. His friend turned the twin-thread screw in the middle of my 'esposas', or spouses, as these manacles are ironically termed in Spanish, injecting thereby into my thoughts the foreboding of imminent extinction, or at best of total reclusion, which led me to volunteer that all this was a gross blunder; we British did not pay ransom or trade hostages – remember my colleague Jasper Cross. Again came the answer 'Quiet!', with its routine accompaniment of a butt end on the nape of my neck, while the butterfly tightened and tightened over my crossed wrists till they lost all sensation. One was to remain completely paralysed for three months, but then became as good as new again, I can only suppose through the body's marvellous capacity to regenerate a severed nerve by some sort of a bypass growth.

Until our unprogrammed pause for the more stabilized insertion of hypodermic needles I had not really had leisure to try to keep track of time, though I should estimate that barely five minutes had elapsed before my change of vehicle, and not much more till the next pause to avoid undue bouncing; through the briefly opened rear doors I had glimpsed an again empty street in, evidently, one of the sad grey suburbs to the north – and I believed east – of Montevideo; the street was wide but the houses grim, of pre-fab type, with small, run-down gardens behind cheap pre-cast concrete fences and walls. From this point to my final destination did not I think take more than another ten minutes. I was able to keep some track of time by counting on the 'one-and-two-and-three . . .' system, and am reasonably sure of my accuracy despite the fact that one or the other of the drugs that had been administered to me was beginning to take effect with that unmistakable head-swimming I recall from my occasional experiences of surgery. Even so, my mind was functioning rationally and, so far as I could tell, efficiently, perhaps because my remonstrations had led to a reduced dosage – unlike the Tupamaros' usual 'one for the pot' liberality with their drugs and narcotics – or perhaps owing to some powerfully personal biochemical reaction, combined with the effort I was making to keep some control over myself and events around me.

For some time the road had been quite rough, and suddenly, with barely a reduction of speed, our vehicle turned off over what felt like a pronounced gully at the edge of the road, rather than the 'mataburro' or donkey-killer, the normal arrangement of pipes laid across the farm-gates in South America to prevent the ingress, or egress, of cattle. Over a hundred yards or less the van swerved in a tight S-turn – right, left, and right again – and drove straight into what, I could see through the handkerchief now held over my eyes, became almost total darkness as a garage-door swung to behind us.

After the tumult of the last twenty minutes or so, the quiet was oppressive, almost sinister. It was broken only by the shuffling of feet, and the creak and thud of some kind of a trap-door. I was hauled out of the van by my arms and my legs and swung and lowered into some kind of a hole not much longer or wider, I could feel, than myself. Having seen photographs of the near-grave in which one of my predecessors had been stored for some time, I protested energetically, though in fact I had already decided that if it came to the pinch no purpose would be served by indulging in claustrophobia. Nothing was said however, and instead, after having been lowered about three feet onto my back, I was edged forward and slid about my own height down some sort of rough ladder. Again I was hoisted by my arms and legs, dragged forward through some sort of a narrow opening, and deposited on not too hard a floor.

The kerchief across my eyes was removed, and around me was a circle of shoes. A pair of quite beautifully cut brown grain slip-ons broke the relative if still hard-breathing silence with the words 'Ay, pobrecito – poor man – What a pistol-whipping he's had – bring me a cloth and some alcohol.' The voice, in a particularly soft, almost lilting Spanish, seemed and still seems strangely familiar; I am convinced I knew it from before. It contained a quality of mirth yet, at the same time, of great evil, though the hand which removed the blood from my brow was gentle, even skilled. From the I suppose somewhat foetal position in which I lay I straightened out. When my feet hit solid substance before my knees had fully unbent I turned my head and looked. By the light of a not too powerful electric bulb I could see at eye-level an expanse of smooth concrete with, above, a conglomerate of rough stone and cement. To my right was a square mesh of strong steel pig-wire, and a timber upright or two. I paused, looked again, and laughed, I like to believe with no hysteria and in pure irony.

PART TWO

GOING UNDERGROUND

Chapter 5

WITH equal amusement, and perhaps even a touch of mock resentment, the gentle voice enquired 'And what, Ambassador, do you find to laugh at in this your present situation?' 'At what looks so like a newspaper picture of a Tupamaro hide-out that it might be a caricature,' I answered. 'Now there's a cool one,' said the voice, to another and less elegantly amiable one which forthwith barked at me 'And who do you think we are?' 'We all know that.' 'But say so, say so, use the word!' 'Of course, the Tupamaros, if you insist,' I replied.

'Now, you have had a lot of hypodermic injections,' intervened the first voice. 'If you have not had anti-tetanus' – and I conceded I had not – 'then we must inoculate you on account of your wounds and abrasions.' I agreed that I had experienced more salubrious journeys, and my interrogator complimented me on my high spirits, which I told him were aptly described in my own language as 'whistling in the dark'. He commented that he could not blame me if I were a little tense, and that he proposed to administer one more 'shot' to relax me prior to the interrogation which I must expect. He did not deny that it would be some such drug as scopolamine, and I warned him again to be very, very careful. Again too I felt no undue reaction, and unless the drug induced some state of euphoria which misleads my recollection, I am reasonably sure that it never wholly dominated me. I had thought out in advance what I might do if ever exposed to this situation which, I realized, could be potentially most dangerous for my government, by perhaps eliciting from me the kind of subjective internal political commentary which is a diplomat's nightmare. So whilst I thought, I decided to divide my ideas into two categories, those unimportant, on which I would be fluent to the point of verbosity, and those on which I would blur my

39

answers until they too reached a point of eloquence which would make the two categories indistinguishable.

Once again my sleeve was rolled up, and the incessant Tupamaro needle ran into my arm. I must have dozed briefly, for I remember being awoken by an insistent tug at the little finger of my left hand, and snarling like an animal when I realized someone was trying to take away my signet-ring. At two quite different levels I felt a sense of utter outrage. It would have been hard to think of any possession of greater emotional significance to me. The ring had been made to replace that of my father, who died in 1938, and of whom my only tangible souvenir had been stolen from me in Egypt long ago. It was made from gold melted from the broken chain-bracelet, many generations old, of my wife's dead mother, of whom I had been particularly fond. The emblem it bore had been supplied to me by my own mother before she died. And the whole ring had finally been a gift from my wife. Fortunately, being an inveterate swimmer, I had had it made tight enough to wear even in cold water; a knuckle conveniently broken while skiing meant that I had only to crook it slightly for its removal to be impossible.

My cuff-links had by this time gone, as had my wallet and wrist-watch, but being by now wide awake, if truth-serumed, I was ready both for my interrogation and to defend my remaining few, small but important possessions. My cigarette-lighter and case were, to my surprise, set on one side for me, on the bottom beam of my cage. But my corpse-robber was not satisfied; and this was the second level – I found myself with Schubert's song 'Die Kraehe' going round in my head – at which a furious disgust came over me, at the thought of corroboratory keepsakes piece-mealing back to distress my wife. When he demanded my True Cross and its chain, on which I was lying, I told him that for this he would have to fight. The soft voice commented, with a curious mixture of derision and grudging consideration, that I might as well be left with my fetishes; this was a point on which we were to come to terms later, though I knew at the time that they were more concerned with the chain than with the Cross, that at the back of their minds was the cruel strangulation of the unfortunate Quebec minister Pierre Laporte only a few months before, and that somehow this concern was obscurely reassuring for me.

Though still prostrate I had by this time looked around me, to find all my company wearing Ku-Klux-Klan-style white hoods. Their purpose, among others, is undoubtedly to terrify. Yet with the curious calm which had invaded me since this upheaval of my existence began I was not in the least intimidated but even mildly amused and faintly disgusted; ever since then I have found newspaper pictures of masked men somehow obscene. As time went by my captors themselves grew oddly self-conscious of their triangular and slit-eyed hood, and a day was to come when they would ask me to restyle it for them.

By this time material preparations seemed to have ceased, and the soft voice went on to question me. Even at the time many of his questions seemed so irrelevant or inconsequential that I wondered if I was not simply being tried out for consistency and for my reaction to a truth-drug. Many questions related to what it was hinted might be my almost immediate return to Britain. Was there a direct flight to Britain from Montevideo? By what line? How often a week, and on what days? I dedicated myself to the consciously verbose type of reply, and flooded them with elaborate detail of British United's current overflight of Carrasco Airport, of our hopes for future services, and such further detail till my questioner wearied and changed the subject.

He wanted to know my views on the internal situation, on the personality of the President of the Republic, and on other items on which, I explained, he simply might not expect a foreign diplomat to comment. I went on to repeat more extensively to them what I had already said briefly during my comfortless transit to my present whereabouts – that as proven by the case of my colleague Cross in Canada, my government did not follow the practice of paying ransoms or promoting the exchange of prisoners; that on this precedent the most they could expect in return for my person was the ultimately self-cancelling outcome of a safe-conduct and their own eventual expatriation; that they had made a great mistake by getting me in their hair; that my government knew that these were my views too, and that my wife would by now already have restated them as hers. Meanwhile I would like to know if my personnel were safe and well after the assault, and for what extremity I should brace myself.

Another and somewhat harder voice replied, dealing with my first question by what I came to recognize as a standard Tupamaro technique, which was totally to ignore it. When I insisted and repeated it he simply replied flatly that he could say nothing about my driver and my other staff. As for myself, I could simply satisfy myself with the certainty that the Tupamaros were not assassins. Definitions, I replied, could vary – he knew it, I knew it, but did the dog know it? And in frankness, I added, precedent was not wholly reassuring for my present case. The voice replied that he was glad that I was facing my problem squarely. It was as well that I should know that, though I would not be murdered, my physical existence could not be guaranteed, in a variety of contingencies.

At this point I decided that there had better be a clear understanding. So far as I was concerned, I said, I was dead already. When I felt two bullets go by me in my car I had got my dying behind me; at this point I should add, the voice effectively apologized, and stated that the young gunman had been disciplined by what I later found was the standard system of taking him off operations and downgrading him in the weaponry hierarchy.

'So you don't mind dying?' enquired anew the soft voice. 'Very much so, but a man can only die once. A poet of ours said "I fear not death, yet fear I much to die," and that part of it is behind me. I'm at peace, my family are safe and will be taken care of. So every moment now is a "yapa", a bonus, the baker's dozen.'

My interrogator was intensely amused. 'So you're a fatalist then'? 'Not at all – just a philosopher.' 'And what might be the difference?' he asked. 'Free will,' I answered, on which he declared that this would suffice for my present interrogation, but that I must prepare myself for another and much more substantial one shortly, perhaps in a day or so. It did not in the event materialize for about a week; this underestimating of time proved to be a pronounced Tupamaro characteristic, going so far as alerting me often for situations which sometimes were, without a word said, never realized.

Chapter 6

My interrogators withdrew and, being at last in a manner of speaking alone, I was able to consider my material surroundings. These were stark; and I was only relatively alone. I was lying on the floor of a small two-sided cage, some two metres broad by a metre and a half deep, built in the corner of a room which itself seemed little more than four metres square, though with a recess behind a screen in two of the corners, and indications of a corridor, and perhaps another room, behind a hessian curtain. The entire floor, including that of my cage, was covered with sheets of yellow foam-plastic. While I had been dozing someone had brought through the door – firmly locked by a long steel cable leading outside – a mattress of sorts. On scrutiny it proved to be very second-hand indeed, being a simple bag of black nylon mesh, filled with polyfoam chips and sewn across into four or five sections. The material was so dirty that my hands were filthy just from arranging it; the fabric was already perishing and the stuffing leaking out – it was clearly going to require attention. There was a woollen blanket but no sheet.

Evidently the blanket was going to be unnecessary, certainly as long as the Uruguayan high summer lasted, which in the southern hemisphere can be until March. Already my quarters were so hot that there was condensation on a spare packet of cigarettes I had with me. So I took off my suit and stripped down to my trunks and singlet, hanging my lightweight suit up on a protruding corner of the wire mesh where it touched the ceiling. The roof was less than two metres high, but effectively not more than five feet owing to a massive concrete beam which ran from the front to the back of my cell; evidently my ceiling was the floor of a fairly massive structure above.

It looked very much, indeed, as if the whole premises had been dug out of the foundations of an existing building which, from their size, seemed larger to me than a mere house would have required. Thus at one point in my rear wall the soil – almost pure sand – was still exposed. The rather amateurish roughcast concrete was brand new, so much so that sticking to the, as it were, skirting-board running uncompleted along the angle of the wall and the floor, almost as far as the wire wall of my cage, were still traces of the newspaper used to line the inside of the wooden form into which it had been poured. Later I was able to detach enough of the paper to recognize advertisements of the pre-Christmas Montevideo sales; so this particular redoubt had evidently been constructed in haste not sooner than some three weeks before.

By now I was lying on my left-hand side, with my back to the larger room, in which three masked young people were moving about. At my feet was my end-wall, the bottom half in smooth cement painted over with a glossy battleship grey down which were running two or three rivulets of either seepage or condensation. The top half was in smooth unfinished cement flat enough, it occurred to me, to mark as a calendar should this situation protract itself. At my head was the other end-partition, this one however of heavy-gauge pig-wire, but with the half nearest the back wall blanked off by a plastic screen to form some kind of a compartment on the other side of the wire; I was to wonder for several weeks what purpose this cubby-hole served and to find out in spectacular circumstances. My face was towards the back wall, the bottom few inches of which – apart from a length of about four feet, all too insufficient as it was to turn out, sealed off by the cement 'skirting-board' – were of naked sand. I felt it. It was damp, but not wet, where it joined my floor, itself also of fairly smooth concrete, as I could see when peeling back the foam-plastic sheeting. Higher up, the wall was made of very coarse and friable concrete mixed with large rough-cut stones, making a very uneven surface, and clearly built in, after the event, to shore up existing poured-concrete foundation members supporting the rough brick foundation of the evidently not too luxurious construction above. Though the air vents in the brickwork had been crudely blocked off, at their very top it was at times possible to catch a cranny of light, presumably from soil-level. Also from the intense heat which the brickwork radiated at certain times it was a fair assumption, what with the further evidence of some almost inaudible birdsong at other hours, that this wall faced west into the blowtorch of the Uruguayan evening sun.

My cage was strongly built, but not so strongly as I would have expected, nor as was to be that to which I was later transferred. The corner-post round which the 'L' of my wire-netting enclosure was angled was set – rather loosely it seemed – into the floor, with its top end simply wedged against the rough ceiling of concrete and steel reinforcing-bars forming a solid floor to the room above. Nor was it so stout that, with a kick or two, it might not have given; not all the wire-netting joining it to the other support was of the heavy-duty pig-wire which was to be the rule in my second gaol, some panels indeed being not much more than chicken-wire. This was the case with the door too, which was quite flimsy, supported on improvised hinges of looped steel wire, opening inwards and held to by the steel cable leading outside to some invisible locking-point. Much of the grille-work was open-mesh enough to put a hand through, and at the bottom a few inches were loose enough for a plate or a cup to pass underneath.

Looking through this front wall of my cage, there was about five or six feet of space with, in the left-hand corner opposite my door, a narrow recess out of which I could see protruding a masked and apparently sleeping head half covered by a hessian curtain. To the right of this was an open doorway of sorts, down which I could see a corridor, then to the right of this some sort of a further partition ending at right angles against another cement wall in shiny battleship grey. Squatting against the hessian-covered partition was a young woman, in jeans and a Tupamaro hood, and standing against the cement wall, against an almost heraldic montage of three sub-machineguns, was a likewise hooded young man. I noticed that the three automatic weapons were all of different types, and went to sleep.

I awoke suddenly and saw in a dim light a rough concrete wall a few inches from my nose. There was no quiet sound of my wife's breathing, and I closed my eyes and opened them again. For a moment of utter horror I realized that the concrete and stone were still there, had not been replaced by the luminous figures of my bedside clock. Only once or twice again in my captivity was its reality to confront me with quite such brutality, just as, since my return to life, only once or twice has the brutality of nightmare so horrifyingly appalled me until my eyes have opened again on the blessedly opposite reality. Yet throughout my long reclusion there was a persistent blurring between reality and nightmare, perhaps indeed to my great good, since I could never truly accept even tangible nightmare as total reality, and even waking retained a second depth of certainty that dawn, and the end of sleep, would disperse even so endless an evil dream.

So, slowly and consciously, I unknotted my stomach, blessed myself and, without deliberation, found myself saying in my mind the one line of the Twenty-third Psalm which, by some odd block, was all that would come through to me for many days – 'Yea, though I walk through the valley of the shadow of death I will fear no evil.'

Sitting up, I saw again a masked head half-protruding from the sleeping recess, the young woman asleep flat on the foam-plastic flooring, and a young man sitting against the partition and reading. I assumed that it must still be night, and in fact it so evolved that two guards took turns during the night to stay alternately awake on watch while, during the working day – if day it was – for much of the time all three were awake, the one who had done night duty taking perhaps three or four hours' sleep as it suited him or her.

'Hola – hullo,' I said, observing that my guard had seen that I was awake; but quietly because of the two sleepers. 'Buenos,' he replied, also softly; in Spanish it is quite normal to greet a person just with the 'good', omitting the 'day', 'morning' or 'evening' in a form almost of elision. But I chose to reply 'Buenos días, if day it is – not that it matters.' He agreed soberly, adding that soon a meal would be available, but if I would care for a cup

47

of tea, he could make me one straight away. I accepted the offer, and he took the top off one of those handled thermos-flasks which the people of the River Plate carry about, tucked under their arm to brew up their maté – an alternative, which in fact my guard had also offered me, though not coffee. Into the flask he inserted a cork with a tubular spout and an immersion-heater element running through it, the whole thing wired to a flex and a dubious-looking wall-connection which, as with most Tupamaro electrics I came to know, inspired me with little confidence. When the steam began to emerge he put a tea-bag into a thick glass and poured hot water on it; it was a later Tupamaro who proved receptive to the significance of boiling water in this ritual. Even so, it made a passable cup of tea, and I was glad of it when he put it just outside the wire, with a tin of sugar, for me to lift it in.

My head was still spinning, if not splitting, and I still felt rather sick. No one had mentioned sanitary arrangements, but by this time they were becoming urgent to me, so I enquired if any such provision existed, or would be supplied. My custodian answered that for evacuation a bucket would be passed inside to me, while for urination it would be put within my reach outside the grille, through which I would have no difficulty in accommodating myself! No suggestion of privacy was made so, internally, I shrugged my shoulders and decided that the habit and convention of these many years were not after all of indispensable importance.

By this time the other two Tupamaros were stirring, and a gourd was produced to make maté; there was only one 'pump' – the hollow spoon-shaped sieve through which the infusion is sucked – which they all used interchangeably. With it they ate – and I was offered – 'galleta', the local hard biscuit which they usually had in its ship's-biscuit manifestation, which kept best. Even this however needed, I was to find, rather special precautions if it was to last more than a day without crumbling with the damp and even growing mouldy.

I had of course no appetite, at which my captors showed concern, which I reassured by warning them that, once I regained it, they would be hard put to keep abreast of it. They said they had orders to ascertain my normal diet, which I explained was of a high-protein low-calorie pattern. My guess, which proved to be right, was that as Uruguayans they would not be able, even literally in the underground, to forgo their traditional addiction to meat, though I would have to be on my guard against their equal addiction to 'pasta' – noodles and macaronis of all kinds – and 'polenta' – a maize porridge with also a high fat or oil content. What I expected to be the difficulty were salad and green vegetables, the first of which they almost always managed to produce, as also the fruits of the season. But for at least two or three weeks I was totally unable to eat, and must have fallen from my eleven-and-a-half stone/hundred and sixty pound normal level by ten or fifteen pounds.

My guard also had orders to ascertain if I liked music, and if so which kind. I explained that I was virtually omnivorous, though I thought that in confined surroundings one could not go wrong with light classical and good instrumental music. I liked popular music, including authentic folk-music, though not protest-music in that disguise; and the only form of music to which I was positively hostile was straight 'pop', which almost physically distressed me. My hosts listened, made notes and, again, when I asked questions, followed their standard practice of ignoring them. There was nothing for me to read, so I too followed my own by now standard practice of not asking for it; already, though unconsciously, I was beginning to formulate in my mind the loose outline of what afterwards I was to reduce to a concise four-point plan of conduct and attitudes.

At the corner of my cell was a bottle of the local mineral water. The unmistakable team-leader of my guards told me that I could drink all I wanted of this, but volunteered that washing was another matter. They would try to let me wash lightly once a day, and sponge-bath once a week, but could not guarantee their facilities; this was after all a People's Gaol, with its own inherent logistical problems.

The forecast was all too accurate. The youthful Tarzan, as I recall, was alleged after eating to 'wipe his greasy hands upon his nut-brown thighs'. So too was I to do, on my own increasingly pallid limbs, often for two or three days in succession. Meanwhile I strove to keep my fingertips more or less clean with a few drops of my precious drinking water. My black-rimmed fingernails, and the greasy patches on my bare thighs, would await the intermittent luxury of the grime-crusted green-plastic 'palancana', or communal wash-bowl, and its sodden little checked towel, after one, two even – in times of duress – three days of deprivation.

It was also explained to me by a later batch of gaolers that as a People's Prisoner I was entitled to urinate once daily, but that out of consideration for the notoriously weak sphincters of middle age there would be for me a special additional dispensation. Its effect was in practice the opposite; I drilled myself, even to the extent of fluid-intake, to urinate once daily only, so long as these conditions prevailed, which was happily not for too long. In any case I could not bear to ask for and see the filthy communal slop-bucket swung over the faces of sleeping 'comrades', in spoon-formation on the often crowded floor. Meanwhile these implementations of sanitary procedure, and an ultimate emergence into salubrity of a sort, lay in a still uncertain future.

Chapter 7

FOR many days nothing seemed to happen. I was able to count them by, at first, making surreptitious lines with my thumbnail in the softwood of one of my cell-beams. Very soon I had realized that my captors had a system of playing the accordion with time, lengthening and shortening my days arbitrarily, presumably as part of their technique of leaving me suspended in time and space with no knowledge of the outside world and its events. In practice their system did not work, first because – when my appetite finally returned – lack or excess of it told me whether the hours had been lengthened or diminished, and anyhow, over a period of days, they tended to balance shortening by lengthening, and vice versa.

In any case, it is hard to deceive the human organism especially when – as in my case I suppose – it has the regular habits imposed by early and sustained training! So, being blessed with a most regular intestine, I kept track of the days to such effect that, three-quarters of a year later, I returned to the world only a day and a half out of true. Once I felt surer of my ground, I detached a large wedge-shaped pebble from the rough concrete of my back wall, and used it to transfer my existing calendar to the flat cement of the end-wall, which I then kept up to the extent of marking the Sundays with a cross so that I should not miss Mass, which I followed in my mind. I had prepared myself for the remonstrance which inevitably came from my guard, and so declared that, far from being a mere calendar, this was a hygienic record of importance, any questioning of which should, I claimed, be submitted to the Tupamaro Medical Corps, or 'Commando Sanitario', a body of considerable hierarchical standing in the 'Movimiento de Liberación Nacional', as the Tupamaro movement is alternatively called.

My contention – which was essentially true – carried all the more weight since, from the first day that I felt well enough, I had set about a steadily intensified programme of physical exercise, aimed at bringing me back as soon as possible to my till recently quite high 'rung' on the ladder of the Canadian Air Force '5-BX' exercises, slightly modified in terms of my particularly cramped surroundings, and as befitted a man in his middle fifties. With very little change they adapted well, the main handicap being that the concrete beam cutting across the two-stride length of my free space was just the right height for me, more than once, to gash either my forehead or the nape of my neck. Still, the jogging-on-the-spot which is part of the system was eminently adapted to this involuntary immobilization, the only difficulty being that, unless I supported myself lightly by my fingertips, some optical effect due to the extreme nearness of my eyes to the beam caused me to lose my balance. Oddly enough, the exact converse applied when I came home, and found my head spinning as soon as I tried to move in an open space; it was three months before I could run for a bus. I even then only rediscovered the ability by running out of the way of a London No 11 rather than after it, which leads me to wonder whether the cause was not after all some eventual psychological agoraphobia rather than a muscular, much less optical, phenomenon.

A far more serious handicap for my exercising was however the rapidly deteriorating condition of my floor, on which a good part of my contortions were practised, prone either on my face or my back. The foam-plastic had within a day or two become completely soaked, its sponge structure drinking up the intense condensation which steadily collected and ran down the painted end of the wall, the alarmingly increasing seepage spreading from the exposed soil at one end of my back wall and, I was mortified to observe, the sweat and dirt from my own feet and those of my gaolers. Soon the flooring had become so sticky and foul that I rolled it back and exercised on the bare damp concrete. From memories of the Persian Gulf, I reckon that, for several hours of the day, the temperature was not less than a hundred degrees Fahrenheit, with a humidity above the dew-point, to judge by the way my cigarette ration beaded with sweat. Only – I suspect – did the considerable movement of the air, force-draughted by powerful compressors, make this atmosphere habitable, let alone tolerable.

This ventilation system was ingenious. From the frequent, almost incessant movement of footsteps above my head I began to assume that the space above was some sort of a public or communal place. The Tupamaros, with their rigorous 'need-to-know' rather than 'nice-to-know' approach to information, never as a rule volunteered it. Later however, when we had major drain-trouble from above, I was able to make certain useful proposals which led one of my gaolers to explain that the room above was a urinal – I have always assumed of a school or small factory – into the ventilation-grille of which the air-vent of our fresh-air system was ducted. He explained that our 'exhaust' was so fetid that to have vented it at, say, an outside wall would have attracted the attention of any passer-by. As sited, its odour was authentically screened.

These material difficulties were to grow, at least in my first dungeon, by an exponential curve, at the start of which however neither my gaolers nor I had really contemplated them; the process of adjustment to a new existence tends anyhow to distract from its anxieties and discomforts. Within a couple of days I was informed that 'my' music had arrived – a cassette-player with a small library of spools most of which I welcomed, but which my guards firmly appropriated for themselves. I was never allowed to operate it at my choice, and at this stage the volume was kept so low that, at my end of our cave, it was practically inaudible to me. My favourite cassette comprised four Beethoven piano concertos but, to my real sorrow, it broke within a day or two. One of my guards, quite a handyman, actually spliced the tape with a knot, but the improvisation did not last long. In general I began to form the conclusion, which the passing months bore out, that these young people were unbelievably slap-happy, casual and heavy-handed with these communal items, no doubt because they were requisitioned, if not 'expropriated', and replaceable.

So records, when we eventually received a player, would often be silenced by a thrust from a foot, scratching irremediably a beautiful and comforting piece by Vivaldi, for example.

Even so, it grew interesting to see how, with successive gaolers, their musical taste evolved to a nearer approximation to my sedater own, which always they began by viewing as rather dull, indicating so with good humour or overt irritation, according to particular temperament. In reality, my musical taste is catholic and rather middlebrow, but tends I hope to nourish without nausea, unlike the protest-music, the synthetic folk-lore and the raw 'pop' which time after time I watched my gaolers grow out of with the repetition of the passing days, more prolonged of course for me than for them. There are things which man may eat three times a day for seven days a week, and not only thrive but take unfailing pleasure from them. To have a terrorist acknowledge this to me of 'Juan-Sebastian' Bach is, I believe, a human truce of sorts which that great soul will not, I know, hold against me from among his sounding spheres.

My next human contact was not however of so generous and consoling a nature. It was the visit, delayed a week or more, of the interrogator foreshadowed by my soft-voiced friend on my first arrival in their underground world. I believe in fact that this second visitor came twice to see me in fairly swift succession. For I had meanwhile reached a *modus vivendi* with my gaolers that, even though their orders were to leave me with no sharp or metallic objects in my cage, a literal if Nelsonian interpretation might suit us both. It would thus be a humiliation for me to ask them for my Cross every time I wanted it, and a nuisance for them to pass me my ball-point pen every time I required it too. So both by this time were hung on a nail on the outer side of the corner-beam of my cage, where I could see and reach them as I wished. With the pen I had started to scribble – to begin with on the captive's traditionally husbanded toilet-paper – a diary so sketchy as to be a mere memorandum. So I remember vividly the successive annotations 'Visit' and 'Visit In Depth!' relating to my current caller.

The first time the young man had stayed briefly. He remarked that 'they' had decided that my mind should be occupied, so I was to draw up a list of the principal local British firms and businessmen, indicating their main activities, wealth, associations and governmental contacts. I had replied that, with the current wave of terrorist attacks on factories and offices, it was not for an ambassador to do their market research for the Tupamaros; they were obviously well equipped with investigational personnel – let them do their own work. The reply was that this was an order, to which my reply was that I took orders only from my government, on which stalemate we parted.

When the same interrogator returned he was in a formidable rage. 'Jackson!' he began – I gather that it was an order from the top that only my surname should be used, though many of the young Tupamaros seemed uncomfortable addressing me so; and after I told them that I would not insist – in present circumstances! – on being addressed either as Ambassador or as Excellency, most of them took to calling me simply 'Amigo'. But my present interrogator was one of the minority among my captors on whose part I thought I sensed a real and personal acrimony. He had for his medium though quite solid build a deep and resonant voice with – for me – a jeering quality, matched by the expression of his eyes and the thick lips of which I believed I had, through the hood, recognized in one of my women guards the female family equivalent.

'Jackson', he stormed, 'you have underestimated us, badly, very badly. Why do you think we have taken you? Answer, say why!' 'Initially for ransom, or for exchange,' I replied. 'How stupid do you take us for? Think again, think again!' 'To leave egg on the Uruguayan Government's face,' I suggested this time. My inquisitor calmed down a little. 'Do you think that your government will exercise pressure through its accomplices to put in turn pressure for your release on Pacheco?' (President Pacheco, the then Uruguayan Chief-of-State, was particularly detested by the Tupamaros.) I answered that, once again, they had miscalculated my government's reaction, and the views of my family and myself. He grew irascible again. 'For you we have reserved quite another destiny! A very different destiny indeed!' I could only assume that my function had evolved into one of a purely public-relations nature, intended to 'polarize' Uruguayan opinion, as their own jargon has it, and to serve ultimately as some sort of a lever to help to topple President Pacheco. I could – and can still – think of no other possible purpose that I might serve, and was filled with misgiving at the prospect of the long wait which might lie ahead while my captors registered their error, and of the scope for irretrievable instant blunder which its strain on their patience might imply.

My optimism was taxed further when my catechist announced that I was an enemy of the Uruguayan people, having shown myself an opponent of the Tupamaro movement. On this I demanded that he should substantiate his words. Because, he declared, I had shown myself friendly and co-operative to the tyrant Pacheco. I thanked him for reassuring me that I had well fulfilled my mission to Uruguay; my government's purpose in sending me was to cement good relations with the elected and recognized government to which I was accredited. My accuser, as by now he was, trumped me by thereupon announcing that they had a full dossier of my anti-Tupamaro attitudes from meetings of the Diplomatic Corps, at which they had friends. I commented that he and his associates were at liberty to credit any hearsay and gossip that they might pick up at any number of removes; but I would agree that, at formal meetings of the Diplomatic Corps, they would never hear me standing up and applauding a movement dedicated to the overthrow of the government to which I was accredited. Even my reports to my own government must clearly, he countered, be falsifying the truth, otherwise my government would have withdrawn recognition from so perfidious a tyranny. I explained that the British Government followed extremely objective criteria of recognition, none of which President Pacheco had infringed. In that case my anti-Tupamaro bias was clinched, my inquisitor crowed, because any honest man would then have resigned his mission as a gesture of moral disapproval. Patiently I explained that British diplomats were serving officers, like soldiers, and their presence simply might not be interpreted in shades of moral approval. Nor, any more than a captured soldier need supply more than his name and number, was I prepared to discuss the substance of my mission.

As so often happened with my captors, at this point the mood of my interrogator completely changed. All very well, he remarked; I was defending myself competently and professionally. But I had given myself away in other ways. Going through my wallet he and his colleagues had found my membership-card of the Montevideo Golf Club – one of the most idyllically situated courses in the world, I should explain, the clubhouse of which has since been burnt to the ground by a Tupamaro incendiary operation. Axiomatically therefore I was an anti-democrat, an oligarch.

This change of pace was providential for me, since it gave me the opportunity to release my tension in an immense guffaw of laughter. The Tupamaros should be thankful, I exclaimed, that the British Ambassador they had kidnapped was an Englishman and no Scot. Any Scotsman would go beserk at the suggestion that golf was an undemocratic game. Even its beginnings were no more than a typically Scottish and thrifty exploitation of marginal agricultural land. I myself had had to wait for twenty years to enjoy a game after playing as a schoolboy on our local municipal links in England, and almost another twenty till able to play again in Montevideo. I simply refused to have ideological strings attached to one of the few sports which a man could play, and benefit from, his whole life long.

Our conversation finished on a strangely affable note. It had, I suggested, rather as our first chat, revealed the Tupamaros' depth of misapprehension where my function was concerned. I had, I said, already made it clear to my custodians that I was not holding out for protocol: 'the Ambassador' did not ask for the communal bucket as such, nor did I have any illusion of 'Excellency' when perched upon it. The substance of my mission was however another matter; and on any point affecting either the interests of my government or my accreditation to the Uruguayan Government, I would pull rank, I would revert to all the 'Excellency' I could muster, and insist on every immunity to which I was entitled, on – or under – Uruguayan soil. On a later and more strenuous occasion I was to have to repeat, almost to renegotiate, this position, that the person was one thing, the institution another. For the moment however my visitor appeared to accept it without further challenge. Over his shoulder he remarked 'Your staff are all right,' and went away.

Chapter 8

ONCE 'His Master's Voice' had imparted this so often and anxiously sought news, there was no need for my duty-trio to remain silent about my driver and his comrades, and I did then receive some news of them, however partial, incomplete and indeed plain inaccurate. What however I most wanted was news of my wife; and I do not think that my own staff will blame me if my immense relief at news of them only whetted further my anxiety to hear of her.

But in both cases an element of imprecison was imparted to the replies of my captors, and persisted until my eventual release. In the case of my staff the story was that only one of them had been 'hurt', the implication being that he had been shot. The truth proved long afterwards to be that all three were hurt, but by clubbing; when my wife visited them in hospital before leaving for England she found Walter so seriously injured as to have suffered a dangerous concussion. Even so, it was a vast weight off my mind to know that none had been killed or experienced any long-term harm.

In my wife's case I simply went on demanding news of her, and whether in turn she had news of me. It was two or three weeks before one of my guards mentioned to me as if casually that she was back in England. I affected considerable calm at the news, and did not pursue it. Later however I mentioned it to my head guard, in the sense of seeking confirmation that my wife should know that I was safe and well. He replied that she did, and that he believed that she would soon be back in England. He was slightly irritated when the other young man explained that he had told me previously that she had already gone and, by a not unnatural reaction, compounded one infringement of the 'need-to-know' system by another of his own. It was in this way that I learned,

not to my surprise, that what he unamiably referred to as a
'cabezón' – a 'Big-head' – from the Foreign and Common-
wealth Office had passed through Montevideo, and had consulted
with the Uruguayan Government; he even gave me his name.
But my greatest comfort was the certainty that, as I knew she
would, my wife had 'obeyed my instructions', as she viewed
them, and gone home, safely away from the pressures and hysteria
which we had seen the wives and widows of earlier captives
endure. She would, I knew, reaffirm my contention that the
British and Uruguayan Governments should stand fast. I had
overheard my captors, in the van which had carried me, tear
apart my briefcase in vain, to the extent of cutting the handle
open to find a non-existent radio-beacon. Added now to this
knowledge that no material source of pressure on me was to hand
came the present assurance that no emotional pressure was possible
either. My captors would have to judge my captivity, my person
and my future on their own strict merits; and for that matter so
now could and would I.

This certainty was a powerful help to me in achieving another
aim. It is an apparent paradox that boredom and fear should go
hand in hand, but a reality that the days were dragging vilely, as
many an ex-captive will recall. Nor did I for many weeks have
anything to read, or visually or tangibly to occupy my mind. But
I had the constant recollection that a friend and colleague had
endured with calm and dignity a prolonged and terrifying ordeal
in Montreal; I had indeed just written to Jasper Cross, only a
few weeks before, to welcome him home to the world of the
living. My first landmark was therefore to hold out for the sixty-
odd days which Jasper had supported, and I shall always be grateful to him for being the first component of whatever process it
was that enabled me to hold together. He was very present with
me. As in so many situations, it is the first step that seems to count,
and when I had exceeded Jasper's unwelcome diplomatic record,
there was still that of Anthony Grey in Peking, whose courageous
response to his own so often repeated self-question – 'What is to
become of me?' – was seldom out of my mind.

As a result I determined to keep a calendar of sorts, and further-more to mark it out so far ahead that my gaolers would realize that there was no pretence in my apparent indifference to my continuing fate, and so report back to the intellectual authors of my predicament whose unseen complicity I felt – and still feel – so powerfully. I could see no logical reason for these master-minds to contemplate my release, if release was to be the end of it all, before at least March of 1972, a year and a quarter away. Only by then would the impending elections have taken effect and, one way or another, decided my position on the Uruguayan chess-board. So, with the sharp stone which I used as my stylus, I re-sited my calendar to where there was space, and prepared a forward calendar which I could advance daily by ticking off an existing mark over the next eighteen months.

At the same time I discovered that the absence of any reading matter till that time had worked prodigies in the evocation of an unexpected capacity for virtually total recall – which since my return to normality has been proved all too sadly ephemeral. To supplement my neolithic calendar I found myself compiling in great detail a daily mental diary. Its main purpose was to ensure that I forgot nothing of value, for a start by not cluttering up my mind with worthless or superfluous items. Each evening, if the moments before my daily sleeping-period may so be termed, I engaged in a process which, depending on technologies, might be termed either 'updating the memory-banks' or 'panning for gold'. There was indeed an element of both; I would record in my memory any event or observation during the day which deserved perpetuation, expunge any earlier item which had either been superseded or negated, and recapitulate the lot. Or I would swirl my mental pan around, as it were, pour away the water and the silt, and inspect what was left carefully for my usual tiny grains of placer-gold or, even, the occasional nugget.

A grain might consist of the discovery that the painful and obtrusive cement beam above my head was so placed that, at certain times, things placed there would tend to dry out; it became a useful shelf for reading-matter when I received it. A nugget was for example the realization that the paces I could hear at times on my ceiling gave me an idea of the area above; though there may have been, and seemed to be, a door or two, I counted twenty-seven steps in one direction and fourteen in another. One grain of near-nugget size was the observation that one of my women guards would sit unconsciously wrapping her toes around her big toe in a way I seemed to recall as peculiar only to ballet-dancers. My greatest nugget, however, was when suddenly I awoke with the words of the whole Twenty-third Psalm entire in my mind. I shall never know by what kind of amnesia anything of such life-long familiarity should have come to be even partially mislaid; so its retrieval was not just the natural solace it was bound to be but, as well, a vast reassurance that my mind and control were normal.

At about this time it occurred to me that the closest approximation to my present experience that I could recall was having scarlet fever when I was about five years old. Then too the days, especially at the beginning, had had a nightmare quality. Then too isolation in confined quarters had been a major part of the process, though transformed and extenuated by the most comforting presence of my two brothers, and the knowledge that our prison was a bedroom in our own home. Then too, after a short time, a routine had become indispensable – the building up and regular overhauling of a little store of personal treasures; the improvisation of a little desk at which to read and write; the division of the day into segments of predictable activity. So, soon, it became in my People's Prison. I would sleep, surprisingly soundly, and so far as I knew without medical aid; only towards the end of my captivity did I accept to take even the mildest tranquillizer, and never a soporific. So when I awoke, I suspect shortly after dawn, I had no difficulty in drowsing off again. My belief that it must have been around daylight rested not so much on the occasional crowing of a somewhat sound-proofed but not too distant cock, a vociferous bird which I have found in practice to be, like the nightingale, a round-the-clock performer and, consequently, a failure at living up to its legend as a timekeeper. Nor was I helped by the muted but nonstop barking of a little dog in the near vicinity.

My real chronometer was the unmistakable dawn-chorus of the birds, faint as it was. I could recognize the aggressive chirping of the sparrows, a regrettable exotic imposed upon the native fauna of the River Plate. Far more agreeable, however nostalgic and saddening, was the sweet and almost inaudible song of the little local song-sparrow, the 'chingolo', a sober, friendly and discreet little bird of which I had become very fond in my own garden.

Not by any means to a majority of the Tupamaros did I learn to ascribe my own version of a sense of integrity. So it came as a sad disappointment to me when it was one of those whom I had come in a way to respect, who robbed me, by a trick, of these sounds of life. 'El Flaco' – Slim – was his name in the Underground, a sobriquet I found applied to or adopted by about half of their number; only very rarely did clandestinity and adiposity seem to coincide. El Flaco had his moments of chatting with me and, on one occasion, he asked me whether, like himself, I did not find these distant dawn sounds a great comfort. I remember quoting Goethe to him, and Faust's tears of joy at the sound of the Easter bells – 'The earth has me back again.' A day or two later there was hammering up above as, evidently, shutters were arranged over the inside of whatever windows were there. Occasionally later, when they were briefly opened, I would hear again a louder noise such as a jet-engine passing over, but never again my tiny but precious dawn-chorus. Next day, when I awoke, 'No birdsong,' I commented. El Flaco shook his head, with regret I thought. 'A pity, but necessary,' he replied. 'Well,' I returned, 'at least now I know what the hammering was all about.' By this time he knew me well enough to expect a joke of sorts. 'What did you expect?' he asked. 'I was just hoping it wasn't a coffin!' I replied. El Flaco laughed, a little grimly, and made no comment.

Not the least in the smaller transformations of my life was that my day no longer began with a shave. I had enquired about the prospects once I had acquired a few days' stubble. My gaolers made it clear that, just as they cut my meat and passed it to me without a knife – at first anyway – neither were they going to put any kind of razor into my hands. I suggested that, for both contingencies, they should have realized by this stage that it was neither of my ethic nor my logic to seek to cut either my or their throat respectively. They suggested that it might be possible for them to shave me every two or three weeks, but it seemed to me that precisely that period of stubble and scratch was the most uncomfortable. So it was either all or nothing; and at least a full beard did not itch, I found, as the endemic water shortage of my first prison became more and more acute. When, on transfer to my second gaol, a photographer was sent to take pictures of me with the Tupamaro five-pointed star emblem, I realized that my half-naked and bearded figure would distress my wife, so I agitated for electric shaving facilities which, in the end, were granted. But at the beginning I had to content myself with a tremendous beard, which at least felt more comfortable every day, which to my surprise and relief was not bright ginger, and which my custodians told me looked 'like the pirate Drake', as he is, alas, still called in South America.

After my morning awakening the first sound I usually heard was the footsteps above which, by their timing, belonged to someone whose first task was to go out and get the day's supplies; he was usually back within fifteen minutes or so. I was then told to turn my face to the wall, while the large communal sanitary bucket was wrestled out of the cubby-hole along the corridor, where my guards could avail themselves of it in relative privacy, and up the precarious step-ladder – a couple of times with disastrous results. The day's newspapers were often there already, dropped down some sort of a mail-chute, or were lowered down along with the day's bottled water and biscuit. Never of course were the papers passed to me. Not until noon, midday, whatever it was, did a second commotion make itself heard from above, with another compulsory face-to-the-wall, when some sort of a cooked meal, the preliminaries to which had been audible from

1. Sir Geoffrey Jackson.

(MVD1) MONTEVIDEO, URUGUAY, JAN. 8, (AP)-THIS IS THE DAIMLER AUTO OF BRITISH AMBASSADOR GEOFFREY M. S. JACKSON AFTER HE WAS KIDNAPED FROM IT BY THE TUPAMARO URBAN GUERRILLA GROUP. CAR WAS FOUND ABANDONED IN THE PALERMO NEIGHBORHOOD, A FEW MINUTES AWAY FROM THE KIDNAPING SCENE. LEFT FRONT FENDER APPEARS DENTED. (AP WIREPHOTO) (JSC612MORGA) 1971.

2. The Daimler.

(MVD--3)MONTEVIDEO, JAN.8(AP)SOLDIERS SEARCH VEHICLES AT ONE OF THE PRINCIPAL ROADS IN THE CAPITAL OF MONTEVIDEO FRIDAY IN ATTEMPT TO FIND BRITISH AMBASSADOR GEOFFREY HOLT JACKSON, KIDNAPPED BY THE TUPAMAROS GUERRILLAS FRIDAY. IT IS REPORTED.(AP WIREPHOTO VIA RADIO FROM MONTEVIDEO)

3. Troops searching vehicles after the kidnapping.

4. Beneath this humdrum-seeming small factory was a 'peoples prison' claimed to have been one of the authors successive dungeons.

5. Only after breaking in was the skilfully camouflaged trap-door to the Tupamaros dungeon found.

6. This cell, supposedly the Ambassadors second prison, had the luxury of plumbing facilities. They were not there in his time.

7. The plank bed of a 'peoples prison'.

8. & 9. Two photographs of the author in captivity released by the Tupamaros. For these posed propaganda pictures he had carefully spread the fingers of both hands in a 'v' sign, but these were screened out when his captors released them.

10. The moment of return—first press conference at Gatwick Airport.

above for long before, was served to us hot. Usually it consisted of quite good cuts of meat, quickly fried up, with green salad and a dressing of sorts, and for the youngsters in charge of me the farinaceous and calorific components their age and growth demanded. The cold remnants were kept for the 'evening' meal.

Given the appetites of the young, the supplies never sufficed. In particular, with frequent logistical and security interruptions, the morning delivery could not, I decided, be counted on. So I started to save up a fall-back reserve of biscuit. I was glad I did so when, more than once, I noted hungry eyes focused on my plastic envelope of reserves, which I could share around when, for as much as a couple of days, food-supplies were interrupted. Just as the average Tupamaro was heavy-handed with communal equipment, so he – and even she – tended to be improvident with their stores. I have often wondered whether this trait had a significance deeper than the question of temperament that I at first assumed; after a while it seemed more than coincidence that all of these young people, drawn together by a common political purpose, should share so identically short-term a view. Ideo-logically, though aiming in theory at a transformation of society, they never seemed to look beyond the apocalypse of its violent upheaval. Studying them about their daily business in their under-ground, I often wondered if the common factor which united them in both a hand-to-mouth existence and a short-range political philosophy was not simply their intense pragmatism, a combination of acute immediate perceptivity with a virtually total deficiency of long-term vision.

Perhaps this analysis is no more than an elaborate definition of the traditional over-impatience of all youth; the fact remains however that, even as their prisoner, I could not sit by and let them go hungry while I kept going on my middle-aged Lan-castrian reserves. Some of my captors evidently viewed my attitude as a trick, or propaganda, and refused to share with me. Others made no pretence that they took it for a sentimental eccentricity, and accepted without thinking or, apparently, remembering. Others, I know, took it kindly. It was perhaps in the mind of the young couple who, when their stint was over, put on their masks again, came back inside, stretched their hands through the pig-wire and asked to take mine. 'You will walk with us all our lives, Ambassador,' were the girl's words. I return them with all my heart, to her and her young man, wherever they may be.

Chapter 9

As I recall, this young couple were the first, or among the first, of my successive guards, who functioned in a constantly rotating team. Its normal quota was of three, usually of two young men and a young woman, and ideally no individual member stayed much less, or more, than three weeks. Usually too there was an overlap of at least one member for some considerable time.

Departures from this pattern were only very exceptionally due to internal and 'domestic' factors; I recall one case in which a guard was withdrawn because the others seemed to believe that he had come too much under my influence, and another in which the young man who was removed had committed a major breach of Tupamaro discipline. For the most part however changes in guard routine seemed to originate in external causes, in that strange other dimension of the outside world which I knew existed but could only surmise from, for example, some sudden influx of personnel indicating pressure, a military sweep, pursuit compelling recourse to the underground. On one occasion I formed the clear impression from the ages, attitudes and personalities of the three young women who joined us, and from the timing and duration of their stay, that they were schoolmistresses lending their services to the organization as a form of holiday task. But particularly at the beginning, in the already cramped quarters of my first dungeon, the rule-of-three was almost invariable.

One slight modification was that El Flaco, second-in-command at first, stayed on a full further three weeks as leader. I have always felt that this was a deliberate choice. He was, I believe, concerned about the next team – very rightly as events were to corroborate. His personality came through very strongly and he was undoubtedly a young man with a strong ethical sense; he took to engaging me in long conversations, usually towards the end of his night watch. He admitted that he was a practising Roman Catholic, he may just possibly have been an ex-priest, and almost certainly he had been a seminarist. He would not admit to being simultaneously a Marxist-Leninist, though he considered this a perfectly reasonable Third World Catholic position. Most of his comrades in the 'Movimiento' were straight-forward Marxist-Leninist atheists, but El Flaco had unmistakable reservations of a traditional nature. Thus, while he had no mis-givings about the right of a priest to participate in the urban guerrilla, he was not entirely sure how to answer when I asked if the finger which held what many believe is the Body of their God might also pull the trigger that would take away a life created by that God.

In some ways these first six weeks of two guard-shifts were more tolerable, though so much more physically distressing, than most of the rest of my captivity, in that special care was, I believe, taken to appoint guards of strong and straightforward personality, prepared to share without complication the extreme physical privation for which I did not even have the consolation of having volunteered. My lowest ebb was to be the last few weeks in my first dungeon, when its material discomforts were compounded by human company of a far baser category than my first gaolers. El Flaco's comrade and predecessor as 'leader' had equally, in his way, been a pleasant young man, prepossessing too insofar as one may judge of a human being without a face. He was known simply as 'Cuatro' – Number Four. Cuatro was no conversationalist, any more than was their woman comrade, the small girl with sufficient vanity to show enough of her face to make it obvious that she was pretty. She also had a practice which I have concluded was a psychological experiment ordered by the Tupamaro command for security purposes. Her weapon was a short ·38 revolver which she carried unholstered in the hip-pocket of her jeans. Given her natural physical endowment the butt tended to protrude and, from where she often lounged or passed in front of my wire, would have been easy to grab. A prisoner with the reactions of a fit young man, and the capacity to kill a young girl, would have had no difficulty in doing so, kicking down the corner-post and reaching one of the three sub-machine-guns hanging on the wall, at certain moments when the two young men were elsewhere engaged. Or so it seemed. In my own case neither qualification existed. In any event I have often concluded, from further acquaintance with the techniques of my captors, their indefatigable cross-checking and invigilation, that I was probably under observation at such times for my reactions.

Perhaps I can forgive the rigours of my first weeks of captivity precisely because there was some trace of co-operation, from my first two shifts of gaolers, in overcoming them. Like myself they anxiously awaited the first delivery of the promised and long delayed reading-matter; they also produced my first writing-materials. My first books were all too undesirably shared with them, for they consisted exclusively of a handful of revolutionary textbooks – Che Guevara's *Guerrilla Warfare*, the essays of Abram Guillen updating it, Marighella's *Minimanual of the Urban Guerrilla*. All were dog-eared and well thumbed and, within days of joining our establishment, mildewed. They made depressing reading indeed, and perhaps on this account I used my first supply of paper to try my hand at drawing, with a borrowed ball-point so as not to use up the cartridge of my own more elegant gold-plated version now clipped to the nail on which also hung my True Cross; I had explained to my guards that I was not disposed to argue as to its authenticity, but that I accorded it the esteem due to any object legitimately revered for at any rate sixteen hundred years, its earlier history being a matter of my purely personal conviction. My first drawing – a most unorthodox experiment in the perspective of superimposed bars and grilles – depressed me so much that I tore it up. I was most disconcerted, and apologetic, when my young lady guard tried too late to stop me, and burst into tears at the destruction of 'a most precious documentation'. So others I did not destroy, and perhaps one day, from some unexpected cache, there will appear some stories and some of my crude cartoons and drawings.

This young woman was replaced at the same time as was Cuatro. He had continued to be only very occasionally communicative, but had indicated that he was of modest origin, had had to struggle for his education, and deeply resented his position as an unwilling drop-out, owing to his enforced clandestinity, from university studies which he suspected he would now never complete. For all his superficial amiability, he nevertheless had a quality of withdrawal – demonstrated instantly at times of danger or crisis – no different save in degree from the virtual schizophrenia which I came to know and, I admit without shame to fear, as the mark of the terrorist.

In contrast, the reassuring aspect of El Flaco, and in retrospect of I hope his deliberate selection as part of my first team of guards, and then as its leader, was his sanity. An excellent professional officer went astray when El Flaco took to the M. L. N. and went underground. During my first few days of captivity the lights of our dugout more than once flickered in the sign that the air-compressors and lighting were about to be shut off, as was standard practice when security forces were in the vicinity. A day came however when the blackout persisted. Suddenly, bearing a torch, El Flaco came into my cage. 'Lie down,' he ordered. I felt the muzzle of his Walther automatic behind my ear. Footsteps marched overhead, returning over and over again. Only long after they had been silent did El Flaco rise from my side. As he did so, his hand gripped my shoulder. 'Real men, you English,' he remarked as he left my cell; though I like to think that the quiet doze I had enjoyed during this episode was the result of conscious control rather than of the sheer nervous shock I suspect.

Cuatro did not reappear one evening. In his place was, in every sense of the word, a strange young man, the first of many who, I was to feel and later to judge, were quite abnormal. He had a voice that suggested some deformity of the mouth, and which occasionally cracked and became falsetto when over-excited. In my own mind I at once named him 'The Frog'. He was pseudo-intellectual, and prone to long dissertations of dubious logic and vocabulary. Physically he was squat and massively muscled. He also disliked me on principle and sight, a fact which escaped neither me nor El Flaco who, while I was supposed to be sleeping, commended me to him earnestly and, I thought, with some concern. I recall the terms well. A very few years ago I should have been embarrassed to repeat them; but one side-effect of captivity seems to be to eliminate embarrassment, whether in the sense of shame of one's vulnerability, or of false modesty before occasional and reassuring achievement. El Flaco explained to the newcomer that he was to go very easy with me. I represented everything the movement hated, but as a person I had many qualities, and merited respect. He should, however, be very careful of me; I was – I heard with some self-satisfaction and surprise, for the first time in my life – 'ferociously intelligent', and attempts to convince me tended to backfire, and work out in the reverse sense.

The newcomer did not sound persuaded, but no doubt as a result maintained during his stay an attitude towards me of wary neutrality, though with one or two quite frightening lapses. With me he talked very little, but the long arguments he had with his comrades showed him to have an abstract and didactic turn of mind which particularly seemed to irritate the occasional instructor who would visit them for indoctrination sessions. These, older men from the sound of them, were unmistakably ultra-orthodox Marxist-Leninists, and disapproved of scholastic extrapolations of dogma which often seemed to lead out towards the lunatic fringe of the Socialist Left. Though The Frog was capable of down-to-earth practicality in the extreme – I had reason to identify in him the capabilities of a competent executioner – he would also occasionally talk himself into theoretical hypotheses of, for example, the post-revolutionary situation which would end in his giggling and piping to himself, to the evident irritation of his companions, culminating once in a stern reproof from the visiting 'theologian'. I viewed The Frog with every possible grave misgiving, and was filled with foreboding when at lights-out one day El Flaco suddenly put his hand into my cage and explained that he wished to say goodbye. He was the last of my gaolers ever to indulge in this reassuringly human gesture, and I returned it by urging him to take care, to try not to get shot, but to return somehow to normality, get married and raise children who could use a good father.

Chapter 10

To say that, with the departure of El Flaco, I knew my good days were over is a very relative statement. Later I was to know in my second dungeon – though again only relatively – much greater material comfort. But never again was I to have the sense, among my guards, of total control and absolute sanity by the definitions of the real world and not that of clandestinity and violence. The absence of his leadership may well have contributed not only to the unmistakable deterioration of internal discipline among the three and occasionally more who dwelt outside my small 'pale', but also to the steady but measurable deterioration of material care-and-maintenance and in its turn of their – and even more so my – environment.

A first symptom of bending rules and declining standards was a radical transformation of our prescribed human relationship. Hitherto my guards had lived and moved, in the L-shaped space outside my cage, wearing their Tupamaro cone-shaped hood, a simple sugar-bag triangle of cloth made from a folded square, and with slits for eyes and mouth. This the new team found insufferable; it is true that the air was daily growing hotter, staler and fouler and, with their chronic carelessness and slapdash maintenance, the lighting and ventilation ever more unreliable. A greater influence was however their undisguised resentment of myself as the occasion of their discomfort. So I was not surprised when, one day, they installed a large curtain made of two blankets across the front grille of my cell, behind which, evidently, they were moving unmasked and in greater comfort. After the 'evening' meal a voice told me to stand by, the blankets were pulled apart and there, squatting cross-legged and huddled against the partition opposite me, were all three of my gaolers. I apologized for going off into a paroxysm of laughter – the old phrase 'like sparrows on a twig' had passed irresistibly through my mind. With slightly sheepish expressions – it is surprising how much expression can filter through a mask – they explained that this was the new ration of human companionship henceforth laid down for me. I was to have one hour of their society per day. I explained that they need not have worried, and that in fact it suited me quite well to be left to my own devices. This response seemed if anything to disconcert them still more; not only evidently was this interruption of my solitude supposed to be a treat but, they admitted, it had been prescribed by their 'comando sanitario', presumably to keep my sanity both in good shape and under observation. After a few days the ritual had acquired almost a flag-raising quality, and I had come to term it 'levantar el telón', the theatrical phrase for curtain-raising. The hour of its duration was used by my gaolers to satisfy essentially their curiosity, professional and even more I think personal, about my thought-processes. Our conversation took very much the form of an interrogation. What were my hobbies? How did I pass my time when not a prisoner? What did an ambassador really do? What was my annual income? Did I own a castle? What size of family did I have? What were their names? How could I justify British neo-colonialism? What did I think of the North Americans? Day after day I answered, simply and with all the matter-of-fact patience I could muster, a myriad questions of this kind. The only comment I ever overheard was that they had decided that my dominant characteristic was my to them prodigious individualism. By the end of my hour's ration I was usually pleasantly tired, and drowsed off. So I cannot say that I regarded my preponderant seclusion as any hardship or deprivation.

Behind the curtain however all was not so well, or so wholesome. The new trio which had formed, led by El Flaco's successor, The Frog, were not of the same category as their predecessors. One young man – I would say at about twenty-eight years rather older than the average – I at once in my own mind baptized 'The Elephant'. He was tall and tending to fat, both unusual Tupamaro characteristics. He was very slightly knock-kneed, and with slightly deformed feet too; I asked myself if there had not been a mild case of polio in his childhood. Even so he was a formidable specimen, with arms that would put to shame many a man's thighs and, above what was already burgeoning into a Falstaffian paunch, a chest and shoulders which did it honour. Like almost all Uruguayans he was well educated, but was one of the few I met in their underground who patently had had no university education. His background seemed to be that of a skilled artisan or technician, and he showed much evidence of a maritime formation. He had read much and widely, but was practical, and enjoyed using his hands; from an old corned-beef can he made a most useful two-way shade, which gave both him and myself enough light to see, and even read by, at 'night', while screening us both from the glare which is one of the most painful aspects of deprivation of normal daylight.

The small young woman was for a while replaced in her turn by another girl of, in all aspects, less delicate attributes. A little on the stout side, she let her I suppose naturally dark hair escape from under its hood to show as a startling yellow. She affected in a variety of ways a deliberate coarseness which profoundly distressed me. In a constricted and unhygienic cavern, group prudery is an unnecessary luxury; but in some strange way the effort stands in lieu of the achievement, and my first woman guard – as most of the later ones of her sex – had deployed an unostentatious modesty which had either fitted in with or set the pattern for a similar unabrasiveness of convention on the part of her male companions. The newcomer appeared to set out with a different philosophy. She encouraged her two companions to use among each other, and in her presence, a degree of spoken obscenity of which I had hitherto had in Spanish only an academic knowledge, though my conversance with River Plate argot was in practice much greater than my captors were till my last moment with them aware. Worse still – to me – she herself joined in with them enthusiastically, and in a vocabularly restricted to a handful of barrack-rooms verbs, nouns and adjectives. And I am old-fashioned enough to feel mortified when, in my presence, a

young woman asks a young man to pass her a plate, or to switch
on the lamp, in a stream of Latin American equivalents of the
Anglo-Saxon four-letter substitutes for the objects and actions in
question.

For the first and last time too in my captivity, thanks to this
young woman's conscious approach to her companions, there
was an end to that unselfconsciousness in matters of hygiene
absolutely indispensable for comfort of mind, let alone for
physical health. She made a point of withdrawing with much
commentary to the guard's cubby-hole, in which the communal
bucket resided, when not increasingly grudgingly hauled out for
loan to myself, there to urinate with a noisy explicitness attracting
facetious comment from The Elephant and his companion. I have
read that this manifestation of sexuality is in essence a form of
flirtation, and was ready to shrug my shoulders at it with indifference – even tolerance, for it is my impression that many a
young Tupamara woman has gone underground in pursuit, even
in search, of a Tupamaro boy-friend. But, also for the first and
last time in my captivity, I allowed myself to lose my temper
wholeheartedly the day that this woman guard indulged her
wit and vocabulary at the expense of my own temporarily
deranged digestion. For most of my immurement I enjoyed
phenomenally good health, especially in respect of the food-
poisonings and intestinal infections to be expected in a setting of
great filth, and when the hand that has squashed a cockroach may
not perhaps be washed till three days later. But dysentery when
once it strikes is neither an elegant nor a euphonious predicament,
and its victim is best left ignored. When the young woman in
question vociferously and at some length drew attention to my
already sufficiently public condition I rose in my wrath. What
angered her and all of them was my venturing to address a
'comrade' as 'child'. But I seized this opportunity to go over
wholly to the attack, and announced that it all was part of a total
change in attitude and treatment against which I wished a formal
protest to be lodged with their 'comando político' – their highest
decision-forming body.

So out of evil came in fact, for me, much good. My guards took my point; and I was thus able to withdraw substantially from them, at what turned out to be a critical moment. Their own over-close association was already demonstrating itself as more than they could handle. Even more so was this the case when the latrine-humoured woman guard was replaced, by another but infinitely more unstable version of 'El Flaco'. This at all events was his official nickname when first he joined the team; but very soon he was habitually addressed as 'Loco' – 'Crazy'. I had noticed that quite often my guards called to each other in this way almost without thinking, much as a young Englishman might say 'Mate' or 'Chum' to a friend and fellow worker. In his case 'Loco' soon became his permanent sobriquet, at first almost affectionately but, as the days passed, with an unmistakable edge to it. Physically he was lean and long-muscled, strong, swift-reactioned and, from his behaviour with his group, quite fearless to the extent of total recklessness; I do not believe that he ever took any action with prior consideration of its possible consequences.

For some reason the curtain had been up when El Loco joined us, and masks were being worn. I had heard it being explained to them that later there was to be a practice-session with their weapons – a form of 'naming of parts' which provided an incessant metallic accompaniment to the normal background din of my first Tupamaro reclusion. Skill with their weaponry proved to be a top priority, with constant disassembling and reassembling of a wide and in some respects motley collection of fire-arms; and some of them – including the young women – were impressively competent at the task. Others, and of them most so El Loco, may have been superlative marksmen, but handled their weapons with the same hamfistedness and slapdash indifference I had noticed in their general attitude to all gadgetry. El Loco clearly regarded guns as a particularly exciting toy only; the first time I saw him he had taken one of the three standby sub-machine-guns from the wall, had it jammed against his hip, and was slowly pivoting as he sprayed an imaginary enemy with a 'da-da-da' of equally imaginary automatic fire. I thereupon determined to have as little to do with El Loco as our enforced proximity made feasible.

These grave misgivings were not assuaged by my overhearing the constant, and constantly crescendoing, arguments in which he was involved with his comrades. On one occasion he proclaimed his addiction to 'Women's Lib.', announcing that never was woman so equal to man as when both were standing behind a forty-five revolver. I later commented that there was one occasion of still more absolute equality, which was when both were lying dead with a forty-five slug through their brain – but this was not to El Loco himself who, I had concluded, was not rational enough for such a comment to him to be safe. On another occasion he outraged one of his companions by identifying himself with the recent destruction of paintings and other works of art belonging to the 'oligarchy', a practice which it emerged was engaged in not by the Tupamaros themselves, but by one or two associated though peripheral groups. His comrade protested, asserting that works of art belonged to the patrimony of the people, and should be sacrosanct. El Loco's view was that aesthetic considerations had no part in making a revolution – 'When I hear of culture I reach for my gun.' He did not realize that he was quoting, and when told that the late Field-Marshal Goering was the originator of his observation flew into an ungovernable rage.

His angers usually took the form of teasing his comrades; though he never I noticed took on The Elephant. His pattern was invariable. It began with needling, with much exchange of braying laughter which, on El Loco's side, became accompanied by mock fisticuffs of increasing force. There was a clear battle of wills in progress between El Loco and The Frog, whose laughter grew more forced with every tap, until finally, instead of a peal of hysterical merriment, there was a suppressed squeal of sheer agony, after a blow which sounded like the collision of two sides of beef, which The Frog forthwith returned in kind. There was a snarl of rage. Then, behind the curtain, I heard the click and slide of a cocked gun.

There was a gasp from The Elephant; but The Frog, his normally discordant voice from yet more between his teeth than ever, in evident agony told him to keep out of it. 'A Tupamaro who pulls a gun on a comrade is no longer a Tupamaro! You are suspended, and I shall demand your immediate withdrawal and court-martial,' I heard him announce to El Loco. What in any army is the most heinous of offences is in an underground para-military formation at least equally so. Total silence ensued, and not another word was addressed to El Loco till, some time later that day, he left our installation without further sight of him.

So far as I was concerned it was good riddance and, I have no doubt, even more so to his fellows. On one occasion, unwillingly on my part and unwittingly on his, I had caught a glimpse of his face, which had far from reassured me. This was without doubt the long, gaunt, flat-mouthed clown-mask which had leered at me from the reconnoitring old De Soto car the day before my capture. His alienation from ordinary life was mirrored in the complexes which he so uncomfortably deployed in our cramped and miniaturized environment – vociferous hatred of his father, ostentatious reference to his sacrifices for the movement, his capping of El Elefante's seafaring yarns with a lament for his own deserted speed-boat which amounted to an inverted bragging. All these complexes made him both poor company and a potential danger to an underground terrorist movement as well as to their captive.

On more than one occasion our conditions had emphasized the need for a steady nerve and a freedom from neuroses on the part of hosts and guests alike. I was hurled out of a sound sleep one night by a quite shattering explosion, from just behind my head at that, followed by billows of acrid smoke but, fortunately, no further explosion. Some sort of conflagration was undoubtedly taking place in the mysterious 'Bluebeard's Cell' behind the plastic-screened netting at my head. The present crisis at least satisfied my curiosity when the stripping away of the scorched plastic revealed that, for the last few weeks, I had been sleeping with my head a matter of inches away from a major Tupamaro arsenal. Apart from scores of weapons, from stolen U.S. carbines to automatic pistols and revolvers, there were great quantities of assorted ammunition, hand-grenades and gas-canisters. It emerged that the explosion had been contributed by one of a boxful of fulminate-of-mercury detonators which, happily, had not set off a chain-reaction. When things had calmed down I seized the opportunity to lodge a formal request that I should be allowed to discuss aspects of my safety, and surroundings, at the highest level.

A further incentive for such discussions had arisen from the fact that our quarters had meanwhile been three times flooded out, the ensuingly enhanced dampness having no doubt contributed to our recent pyrotechnics by corroding the offending detonator. The outer world had evidently entered into Montevideo's rainy season; just occasionally when the shutters were open in the building above us I had briefly heard the gusting of the wind and the drumming of the rain. The soil out of which our oubliette was dug no longer dried out, but was soaked past capacity; small springs were welling up behind the cement walls with literal mopping-up operations constantly necessary. The exposed sand against my main wall was by now flooded, but fortunately it seemed to drain away into what proved to be the armoury; so I had no more than endemic damp to cope with on my floor, by now as in the whole of our establishment somewhat ineffectually covered with tarred paper.

Twice however we were flooded with storm-water from an overcharged drain. Though inconvenient, and a major task to clear, it was at least clean; but I had my doubts about a large concrete bend near the ceiling, the joint of which seemed to be sweating. One day it burst, and it turned out to be the main sewage-exit of the building above, blocked on its way to the street, and with its contents backing up and finding their lowest level in our dugout. In minutes we were a foot deep in liquidized sewage, and it was a case of 'all hands to the pumps', or at least to the buckets passed down through the quite exceptionally opened trapdoor above. Despite much application of disinfectant, I do not believe that the atmosphere ever lost the aftermath of this uncalled-for intensification of its inherent stink.

Yet with all this I had received two amenities which helped to make all the grimness and discomfort that little more tolerable – books, and a bed. My first book was a Bible, in Spanish, followed shortly by a remarkably ecumenical English version. The British and Foreign Bible Society – whose name I shall always bless – had been at pains to indicate where Protestant and Roman Catholic interpretations were different. My version likewise contained an alternative translation of the Epistle to Philemon which gave me a welcome laugh, as well as torpedoing self-pity, by offering – with an asterisk – the phrase 'I Paul, an ambassador and a prisoner for Christ-Jesus'. At the foot of the page the asterisk explained that for 'ambassador' the original Hebrew offered as an optional translation the phrase 'old man'! Almost my only other book at this time – certainly the only other one I cared to read – was an Argentine translation, serialized in magazine format, of Tolstoy's *Anna Karenina*. I read it time after time, increasingly turning my back on the unfortunate Anna, with her unerring capacity for taking wrong decisions, in favour of Levine who, though almost an anti-hero in the same sense as Pierre in *War and Peace*, yet unerringly sweats and stumbles into the right decision.

The inward comfort provided by these first books was matched by the modest physical comfort provided by my bed, a real bed, received after some weeks, with a similar folding camp-bed to fit into my guards' sleeping-recess. By what to me still rates as a miracle, it proved possible with barely a millimetre to spare to manhandle it into my cage, unfold it, and set it up against the main wall. Admittedly it left me with a strip of floor parallel to it of barely two feet for exercise; but at least I was off the ground by the time the floor was really foul, and the floods came to make it fouler. My camp-bed was flimsy and of lamentable quality and construction, so I set to work to reinforce it, in anticipation of trouble, at its weaker points. By the time it was beginning to sag I was able to replace the interim piece of string holding up its middle, and mine, with a wide band which I had plaited, triple strand next to triple strand, from some rough sisal cord which I had persuaded my gaolers I did not plan to use for an act of felo-de-se. In fact I offered in vain to plait another for them, and did my best not to seem smug the day when, inevitably, El Elefante went off duty and hurled himself straight through their communal camp-bed, to a sound of rending plastic and buckling tubing.

Yet my new camp-bed was to be the venue for some of my blackest hours, on occasion literally so. I am not referring to the 'dark nights of the soul' which, by a variety of means, I was always able to dissipate, though after a while, in my new dungeon later, there was a steady recrudescence of the awakening to pure horror which had marked the beginning of my captivity. I am thinking rather of the various occasions when the lights flickered, switched off and on from above in the unfailing sign of an approaching sweep by the Uruguayan security forces. Within two minutes they would go out definitively, and the big air-turbine would sigh itself to a standstill. Absolute silence and pitch darkness followed; my gaoler was already in the cage with me.

The Leader on one occasion was the young man of the gritty voice, 'The Frog'. I do not know whether instructions for my handling had meanwhile been modified, or whether he chose to interpret them more rigorously than had El Flaco. But he made me sit on the edge of my camp-bed, with my face inches away from the invisible stonework, my knees straddled – for there was little room – and with my arms crossed behind my back for, once again, the infamous Tupamaro butterfly handcuff to be screwed on to my wrists. I swore to myself that I would make no sound of pain, and hold out for the apparent eternity it took for the heavy footsteps overhead to cease, and the sound of vehicles to move away. On that my custodian showed yet again the difference between his quality and that of El Flaco. He chuckled sombrely and said without turning his head, as he pulled the door of my cage to, 'If you thought that you were going to get away with it like your friend Cross, then you have a very wrong idea of our instructions for any rescue attempt.'

Eventually, and for the first time in weeks, I received a senior visitor to whom I was able to amplify my contention that I was imprisoned in a fire trap, among its other hazards. I protested that under no Article of War or Geneva Convention was it legitimate to keep a prisoner sleeping on a munition dump, and that the electrical installation was so unreliable that more than once I had had to endure the traumatic experience of a supposed security-sweep which proved to be no more than a faulty fuse. My visitor accepted these strictures mildly, but pointed out that this was after all a People's Gaol, that like the movement itself it was still of necessity an underground operation, that I was getting the best they could give and, despite my status as prisoner, being treated just like my custodians. He here anticipated me by conceding that they admittedly were present in a voluntary capacity! Before he left however he gave me a clear hint that the Political Command found the material problems of running my present People's Gaol insuperable, and that one solution might be to transfer me to another place. Meanwhile, he remarked drily, I knew as well as he did that I could let myself out of my cell with a single kick if ever there were a real fire emergency. I enquired why, then, all this elaborate system of wires and locks? 'It is all symbolic, as well you know' was the reply. That is as may be; but what kind of a symbol? In similar surroundings later the same symbolism was not to apply; and to die like a rat in a trap might by then have been a real possibility.

Before however I was to meet these new surroundings my 'robber-cave' still had one or two last surprises to reveal. I had not yet given up smoking, though I had already reduced my self-appointed ration considerably. My gaolers faithfully produced a daily packet of the very adequate local Virginia-type cigarette, and El Elefante, in one of his later quite frequent moods of relative amiability, had offered me 'the makings', seeming touched to find that an ambassador, and a gringo at that, should know how to 'roll his own', though needing some advice on technique, which he extended. He had not always been so affable; shortly after his arrival I had heard him, behind their curtain, enunciate to the Leader both that he detested all I stood for, and his readiness to 'pegarle un tiro' – put a bullet through me – any time convenient. And my teeth had also grated, in the heyday of his friendship with El Loco, at his constant sniggering and teeth-sucking about the 'pretty plump little Tupamaras' who allegedly had warmed his couch since his recourse to clandestinity. Aside from these juvenilia however El Elefante had shown himself increasingly friendly, particularly in the matter of cigarette-lighters, of which he had an impressive store. When my own ran out of gas he replaced it instantly with a handsome solid gold model, itself replaced with another when, in its turn, its flint wore out. I had already had my suspicions before our nocturnal conflagration. Apart however from the stacks of weapons its 'open Sesame' had revealed, to be subsequently greased and repacked in heavy plastic, there were half a dozen massive canvas bags, which it was also decided to open for the grading and repacking of their contents. These turned out to be the loot from a recent and most spectacular assault on the State Pawn-Bank. I found their contents most pathetic, by far the majority being small gold lockets, wedding-rings, filigree brooches and such-like trinkets pledged for small sums and evidently of primarily sentimental value. Occasionally my gaolers would ask my advice on a piece, and clearly were somewhat on the defensive about its possession, stressing unduly their contention that these objects were not taken from the poor, but from the thriftless oligarchy. Again as so many times, their lack of *pietas* for ordinary material things upset me deeply, particularly as I saw the more massively precious of these objects – like my string of luxury cigarette-lighters – separated for disposal while the rest, despite their 'fragile' markings, were stuffed back, bent and crumpled, into their sacks, there – as I later saw them – to be sat and even stood upon. But again out of evil was – for me at any rate – to come much good; for I could no longer bear to use a lighter of this origin. So, as was soon to happen, when it became clear that smoking was to be a problem I dropped my remaining self-imposed ration of some five cigarettes a day, and gave them up altogether without the slightest effort or sense of deprivation.

PART THREE

NEW QUARTERS

Chapter 11

Now that our visiting celebrity had let at least the smile of the cat out of the bag my guards were able to use the prospect of my forthcoming relocation as one way of enlivening the tedium of their, and even my days. I would, they assured me, find life very different. My new destination was the Movement's most luxurious 'cuartel' or barracks. Above all, there would no longer be any problem of hygiene. My cell would have its own bathroom, complete with shower and water-closet; we might even go easy on our present exiguous ration with such a prospect of abundance ahead of us.

I knew enough of Latin America, the River Plate and student humour to recognize the familiar 'malicia criolla' when I met it. Yet I can confess in retrospect that my heart beat with an almost childish hope and excitement when one morning – by my time – I was woken early, given my suit and shoes, and told to dress, and to put together all my possessions. Carefully I made a neat bundle of the few papers I had accumulated – the first Spanish outline of the first of my children's stories; the precious read and re-read Bible, and Tolstoy; my pen, inscribed with my name by my wife; the birthday message from her which was my most treasured possession, procured by me in circumstances yet to be described and kept for safety in my by now mildewed and verdegrised crocodile cigarette-case, itself a cherished link with dear friends at home. Thank God, I did not parcel up my Cross but, surreptitiously and successfully, secreted it in my pocket. All these things were tied up with string by one of my guards, who assured me that my other long-unseen possessions – watch, keys, brief-case, wallet and the rest – would likewise accompany me on my transfer. They did not.

The morning and most of the afternoon passed with us all on

tenterhooks for our summons to go. Then came the message – for reasons beyond their control the 'cuartel' could not send for me. The operation was set back by twenty-four hours. But somehow they passed; I slept, was woken, and told to come out through my now open cell-door.

It was with a strange feeling, almost of liberation, that I walked through a door through which, on the only other occasion, I had been carried half conscious. But my elation was promptly snuffed out when, immediately, I was blindfolded and told to place my hands behind my back. Yet again the atrocious butterfly hand-cuffs were applied, tightly enough on my wrists but, above all, with my arms forced into an angle excruciatingly painful to my shoulders, which already were showing signs of calcification. I was led down the corridor and told to feel with my feet for a ladder; obviously I could not hold it so, as I found rung after rung, I was pushed against it from behind lest I fall. After quite a struggle I found myself standing up in what, through the not wholly light-proof bandage, seemed like a large garage. My guards however went through a ritual of frog-marching me around – tromp, tromp, tromp, and through the bottom of my blindfold I could see the thick legs of the gritty-voiced Frog, as he led me through the so often read-of routine, of stooping for non-existent tunnels, touching my head with imaginary ceilings and doorways. At last I was halted and told to stand straight. Over my head was pulled a rough canvas tube like a bolster-case, at which I protested both for my breathing and for my stiff shoulders. The only reply was to be lifted by my legs and shoulders, to be laid down, and to feel my feet slid into yet another canvas bag, round which a coil of rope was spiralled. Again I was lifted, and dropped heavily over some sort of a sill onto the metal floor of a vehicle.

It started up with the greatest difficulty, and stalled with monotonous regularity for the next twenty-eight minutes – again on the one-and-two-and-three basis – to the panic of the driver and the apparent amusement of a cheerful-sounding young man who had instantly pressed the muzzle of an automatic to the nape of my neck, with a corresponding warning to me. He threw a heap of tarpaulin over me, the truck's motor finally caught, there was the rattle of a door and, through my blindfold and two thicknesses of canvas, for the first time in – by my reckoning – almost three months, I sensed rather than saw the light not just of day but of the sun. We were soon in heavy traffic, and the bouncing around on bare steel, with my hands pinioned behind my back, was excruciatingly painful. After a while, and in between counting off the seconds and minutes, I muttered to my invisible guard, whose feet were planted on my back by this time, that I could not hold that twisted position; I must turn over onto my back. He whispered that I could do so before the next military check-point, but that one false move, or sound, and he would pull his trigger. On my back, by intermittently arching on my heels and the back of my head, I was able to take some of the strain and the jolting without too much pain. Worse was the inward pain, the profound grief, of hearing the sounds and feeling the light and warmth of real life slipping so inaccessibly by me. At the check-points I heard young soldiers joking with my custodians – we passed through at least two.

Finally, once again, the truck turned sharply, bounced through a gateway, and down a drive, stopping in some kind of a loading-bay still open to the daylight. I was lifted out, unwound and slid out of my superimposed cocoons, to find my blindfold had slipped so much that I could see clearly from under it. The loading-bay I was in led into a large building, and around me were walking young men in white dust-coats, who paid no attention to a visitor of such unusual provenance; whatever their ostensible function, there could be no doubt that they were privy to what was going on with me. I was led inside, through a door into relative darkness, and yet again the ritual of stooping for imaginary low ceilings and being turned around and around was pursued, though – in retrospect most significantly – I was walked down a couple of ramps but never needed to be lowered down ladders or steps. Finally the light grew bright around me again, I was pushed into a seated position and my blindfold removed.

Chapter 12

To say that I was bitterly disappointed with what it proved was to be my home for some six months more would be an overstatement; I looked around and assessed my new surroundings entirely philosophically. I had assumed that my previous gaolers had been amusing themselves with overlavish accounts of the luxury that awaited me. In any case, on first sight at least, the installation was clean and dry – a good deal more so than I was.

But to offset these advantages were two immediately visible retrograde factors. I had even less space than before, and the structure of my cage was infinitely more solid, the wooden structure being of really massive beams and the wiring all of heavy-gauge and close-mesh pig-wire. The massive door was elaborately bolted, each bolt being additionally secured with a padlock; at its foot was a sort of cat-door held to on the outside by a light bolt; it occurred to me – and I after confirmed it was so by cautious measurement – that in an emergency I might have forced my way out, one arm first, at the cost of some effort and a skinned shoulder and hip.

I was lying on a plank cot some two feet wide which seemed to be hinged against the back wall of my cell. Between its edge and the mesh of the front wall was barely a foot of space so, evidently, to move at all or to exercise I was going to have to hinge up the bed, as also a small table hinged down from the framework of the front wall. I was lying on a hard mattress of raw wool flock sewn into a cover of clear plastic, with a stiff new sheet of rough blue twill and a grey wool blanket. The light-bulb, a very powerful one, was set in a reflector made from the bottom of a large tin can. Outside was a compartment, obviously the screened-off end of a corridor, in which an armed figure sat looking at me through my door. At his left hand was another door; I realized that another cage ran at right angles across the end of the corridor and my cell. Standing looking at me through the mesh was a figure – an un-masked human form, with a face, features, forehead and expression for the first time in how many days? He greeted me by name and by title, while I thought numbly who he might be. The only other terrorist captive of whom I knew was Dr. Claude Fly, the United States soil expert; I had good reason to suspect that Senhor Dias Gomide, the kidnapped Brazilian diplomat, had already been liberated, and was very shortly to confirm this deduction by a most curious accident, if accident it was. Dr. Fly I recalled as a slender and ascetic figure, whereas my new com-panion in misfortune was strongly built and, under some days of stubble, of a full face that was familiar to me. He introduced himself as Dr. Berro, the Uruguayan Federal Attorney, whom I had of course received in my home on a formal occasion.

I found myself profoundly touched by this sudden link with a familiar if vanished existence, and by the great distress which this experience was clearly inflicting on a devoted family man. Equally distressing, to myself also, was the harsh limitation explicitly imposed by our captors on our association; Señor Berro made it quite clear that any conversation other than banalities would have serious consequences for him, and on more than one occasion the harshness of our captors was intensified when, quite innocently, he gave the impression of wishing to convey to me news of the outside world. He had been whiling away his time writing down recollections of his boyhood in the Uruguayan countryside, for which he retained a transparent and deep affection, and I was obscurely offended – and bore it in mind – by the way our captors removed sheet after sheet as barely he finished it. After only a day or two I was ordered to lie down, a ski-cap with padded ear-flaps and a built-in blindfold was jammed over my head and strapped under my chin, and I heard a new and hectoring voice in the next cell, though too muffled for me to follow what was evidently a strenuous interrogatory of my companion. When my 'helmet' was removed the next-door cell was empty. Stronger than my anxiety for Señor Berro's safety – and my regret for his company – were my hopes for his freedom which my gaolers, with uncharacteristic loquacity, corroborated to me.

Almost immediately I was moved from one cage to the next – from People's Gaol Cell No 9 to People's Gaol Cell No 10, according to the home-made hand-stencilled tin label nailed to the inside of each door. The transition was marked by countervailing changes in my surroundings, of which – for a while – the deterioration more than cancelled out the modest improvement. My predecessor's cage had the great merit of being much less of a cage than its neighbour or the one before that; and to a captive even asymmetry can be a condition of amazing novelty and enduring interest. My new installation probably had no more disposable area than I had known before in the Tupamaro environment, but it had at least a corner where I could swell my chest. Built at right angles across the approximate six feet represented by the depth of Cell No 9 and our access-corridor, my plank-bed, or bunk, again some two feet wide with a space beside it of some eighteen inches, in useful length took up only the three-feet width of the neighbouring cell. The rest of its length fitted into a recess for my legs, built into the foundation-walls, or behind a major supporting pillar, of what was evidently a massive structure above. The whole layout, though reminding me ominously of a coffin-niche in any of the leading catacombs of Rome, Highgate or Latin America, should have been quite convenient save that it required a brisk knees-bend on arising, a genuflexion sometimes overlooked when awakening in a daze, nightmare or haste. The result was that I broke a toe against the concrete pillar a couple of times, and in any case, with a top shelf above me, never overcame a sensation of the old-fashioned practice of being 'bundled', if not indeed of premature burial. However, the corresponding advantage was that my free space was L-shaped, at the head of my bed being a rectangle the width of my door – some three feet – and the depth of my bed plus its 'bed-side-carpet' area – some three and a half feet. In it was a drop-down table of a really useful size which also, hinged up, left good room for my jogging and bending – though not my floor-exercising – plus the bonus of being able to take two consecutive steps, a right turn around the corner of my bed, about turn, and back again. I could at last go for a walk.

Yet it is all too seldom that the captive's childish though always hopeful pendulum of profit and loss comes to rest evenly in the middle. A compensating and for a while disastrous change in my environment occurred to make me almost regret my enlarged *lebensraum* in favour of my earlier squalor, by now much reduced. For no evident reason, and with total suddenness, I found myself deluged with sound.

From the beginning my new environment had been acoustically much more sophisticated than the first. Behind the numerous plastic curtains was evidently a large and complex barracks installation, with a ventilation system to match. The incessant roar of the air-turbines, never reduced save during a security-sweep or, to some extent, during sleeping-hours, was less bother than might have been feared; after a while the ear discounted it. Nor had the unseen loudspeakers – which I soon located behind the plastic sheeting at the head of my cell – at first exacerbated me, with their nonstop airport-type background music so admirably once characterized as audible wallpaper. But from one moment to the next its volume was stepped up to a degree which – to me at any rate – was physically painful. Even the music that I loved, let alone the crudest 'pop' which I now as a result abominate, reverberated and boomed so that my head itself pulsated.

I let some time pass to see what I could make of this procedure, and of its duration. When it seemed that permanence was of the order I signalled to the guard perched on his stool in the curtained-off square at the end of the corridor giving access to both cells; the loudspeakers, I had ascertained, were pointed inwards to my zone and away from my captors'. I asked him to turn the volume down; he said not a word, vanished for a moment, returned, and placed a fistful of cotton wool through the cat-door which was the normal access to my premises.

By this time I had learned – or decided – not to assume that gestures of this kind by my captors were axiomatically meant as acts of deliberate malice or cruelty, and was deliberately not hypersensitive in my interpretations of them. It proved to be a wise approach and, I believe, spared me much unnecessary self-torture. There is no purpose in imagining deliberate cruelty when either it does not exist or, if it does, is inherent in the situation rather than arbitrarily superimposed on it. Only occasionally in my captivity did I meet personal cruelty with the unmistakable reek of malice or sadism identifiable with it.

So when I stolidly and without protest stuffed my ears with the proffered cotton wool and found that the external din seemed to be transmitted by the bones of my head rather than via the eardrums, I simply so commented to my duty-gaoler rather than complain. He reacted positively, saying that he had an idea, and within one noisy and endless day's time had produced a little box containing some rubber ear-plugs. Regretfully I pointed out that these devices were for athletic rather than acoustical purposes, being for swimming and containing their own built-in tympanum, precisely to keep water out but to let sound-vibrations through. He had better, I suggested, consult the 'comando sanitario', or medical corps. Presumably the purpose of all this discothèque-style din was simply, I submitted, to serve as an acoustical screen between myself and their own surrounding activity, rather than progressively and consciously to injure my health, which it was bound to do. Some measure of compromise was essential which I thought must be worked out between their different services. Within twenty-four hours the volume of the music was reduced to a tolerable level and, during the sleeping-period, actually switched off. To me it was the end of a true physical torture.

I have often suspected that this period of great discomfort and unhappiness may have been due to sheer thoughtlessness in the world without. From certain reactions of elation and excitement among the custodians of my first dungeon I had concluded that my unseen Brazilian and American fellow sufferers, wherever they had been recluded, were now at liberty. That my Brazilian colleague was safe at home I discovered when trying to rearrange my plank-bed, which I found lined with quite recent newspapers. I have often wondered whether these had been left by total accident or to try me out; the fact is that by a prodigy of speed-reading, repeated after what I hoped would be a couple of safe intervals, I had extracted the gist of Senhor Dias's release, which gave me great comfort. It emerged later however that he had quite naturally disclosed at the official level many of the small techniques which any captive devises to secure and piece together odd scraps of information; techniques however which not all of his immediate milieu had been discreet enough to keep to themselves. As a result instant measures were taken to prevent the discovery and use of similar techniques by myself; in general my much longer stay in my second dungeon was in consequence far less informative and informed than my first stint. It seems to be a fair assumption that any point scored off the urban guerrilla underground by one victim is reclaimed implacably from the next. Governments, media, family and friends, even the victims themselves, will do well to remember this harsh reality in the euphoria of new-found freedom.

The signalling of this fact enables me, by now without any such risk of jeopardy, to revert to the one merit – the acoustical – of my cramped and unwholesome first quarters. There overhearing was not a matter of eavesdropping, and on more than one occasion I blessed the facility. I had gathered that my hosts had taken more Uruguayan prisoners and, on one occasion, I had heard them occupied, with some visitors, in what sounded ominously like a kangaroo-court *in absentia* on one of the new captives well known to me. They particularly detested his philosophy and way of life, and El Elefante formally proposed his execution. In horror and outrage I heard myself shout through the curtain that precisely as Marxist-Leninists they might not commit so irrational an atrocity. To my equal amazement I heard my outburst accepted with a laugh, and a mild invitation to continue.

I asked if I could assume that all present if invisible were indeed Marxist-Leninists. They acknowledged that they were. In that case, I contended, they of all people must accept that man not only moulds but is moulded by his environment. By all their own definitions their new captive's particular characteristics to which they took exception must be presumed to be the product not only of heredity and choice but of his childhood, of acquired physical characteristics, even of particular traumatic experiences. They listened with apparent interest, and conceded that by their own logic the contention had merit. The captive in question is alive today, thanks to a tenacity and valour almost inconceivable. But I like to think that this strange subterranean advocacy, sight un-seen, may have contributed a material stay of execution, however small, to his survival.

If in this way I helped another captive, the small altruism expended will not, I hope, be diminished by my unashamedly selfish joy in the greatest personal milestone of my long solitude when again, thanks to luck and the favourable acoustics of my otherwise atrocious first gaol, I had been able to achieve the one and only certain contact with my wife, and my family. This was the birthday-message, the treasured preservation of and heart-breaking separation from which I have mentioned along with my 'packing' for transfer to my new premises.

I had long noticed that at a given hour, from behind the blanket-curtain, I regularly heard a thump in the 'mail-chute', followed by a lull in conversation and much rustling. So came a day when, after careful checking with the 'calendar' scratched on my wall, I cleared my throat and asked just when someone was going to read my wife's message to me. An incredulous total silence followed, then, after some hasty further rustling and time to don masks, up went the curtain. Just what did I mean, I was asked.

It was, I explained, my wife's birthday-telegram that I had in mind. It was undoubtedly in their morning papers. My wife was quite incapable of failing to seek to put a message through to me, wherever I was. And the Uruguayan press would quite certainly consider it of sufficient human interest to relay it. In any case today, the fourth of March 1971, was my fifty-sixth birthday, and merited the modest present of having it read to me.

The team-captain – it was no longer El Flaco – did not hesitate. He commented that in such amazing circumstances he did not feel obliged to consult higher authority or follow channels. He disappeared behind the hessian screen towards where I assumed they kept their stores and a bathroom of sorts, and from there read out aloud, in Spanish, the following laconic but to me infinitely eloquent message:

'Without any news of you on your birthday we all send affectionate wishes for your good health, with love and kisses from all the Jackson and Delany families. Evelyn Jackson.'

Trying to conceal the wildest state of exhilaration I had till then felt in my life, I thanked the team-leader, and added that I would ask two further kindnesses. The first was a copy of the newspaper cutting for me to keep and re-read, the second was his acceptance of a reply for transmission as convenient. He replied that on both points he would require authority, but undertook to put the matter in train. At the end of March a British pressman telephoned to my wife from Montevideo, to tell her that the Uruguayan press had just published the following letter from me:

'Evelyn Darling.

I must write these brief words to you in Spanish.

I receive no news, nor have I been able to send any. But, darling, your wonderful birthday message was read to me. It meant everything to me, especially to know that you are with the children.

I worry about your health. Mine continues well. I eat a healthy diet, drink a lot of tea, keep my mind and spirit very active, and likewise my body with 5BX exercises. So my morale keeps very high.

I won't upset you, darling, with endearments inevitably public, and best kept for our reunion. You know my heart as I know yours. Meanwhile all my love, likewise to the children

97

and all our dear ones. Keep faith and confidence, and always rely on the Old Firm (HMG).

God bless you.

With kisses and all my love,

Geoffrey.

P.S.   Please, would you confirm with United Services Insurances of Winchester that both policies – car and effects – are up-to-date.'

I had a blind and intuitive confidence that this message, complete with deliberately reassuring trivia, had been delivered, unlike others that later, I asked – or was asked – to draft. That certainty supported me during the long months that were to follow. Such direct human contacts as those months were to offer had, all of them, their own nightmarish quality, even though one such contact was to bring me the companionship of as fine and brave a man as I have met in a lifetime and a world's space.

Chapter 13

THE nightmare was however to continue unshared for a while, before Ricardo Ferrés came by his company at any rate to alleviate it; for to dissipate it totally would have been beyond human capacity. At its very best my involuntary speleology had a nuance of surrealism, sometimes even farcical but always sinister, and oscillating at its most evil towards a quality of the Dantesque best conveyed visually by Hieronymus Bosch and verbally by Wyndham Lewis in his *Childermass*.

This element of tantalization, even however mysteriously of the purgatorial, grew more and more intensified as, in my new surroundings, I was tipped off that, any day now, I was to be interviewed by a 'top British journalist'. Eagerly, anxiously, I began to examine, discipline, even rehearse myself. I had no illusion that a correspondent of *The Times* or *The Guardian* – for some reason these were whom I was induced to expect – would have fought his way only with greatest difficulty into so subterranean an encounter to discuss themes of mere human interest. I was, quite frankly, deathly scared that my last few weeks might have softened me into a forgetfulness of what I insistently knew I still was – Her Majesty's Ambassador. So, though my current ambassadorial uniform only consisted – according both to my memory and to newspaper texts I subsequently was to read – of a pale-blue cotton swimming-trunk and a bright pink shirt of coarse twill, I determined to make the most of things in asserting my professional identity.

For the good of my subterranean soul I had lately been given to read a book which – I had not the heart to say so to my gaolers – I already knew inside-out, had read repeatedly, admired and even perhaps unconsciously as a would-be fellow craftsman envied – *Cien Años de Soledad* – 'A Hundred Years of Solitude' – of

Gabriel García Márquez. Utterly as I detested his rancour and negation, I could not but marvel at his craftsmanship and his rendering of a country which I know and love so well. To be given, so purposively and urgently, a book which I already knew intimately, loved, disapproved of, had on my bookshelf at home in a saner lost world, and have at my elbow today, filled me with both comfort and, almost, derision, save that never have I nor shall I deride another's convictions, however I may deplore them. I was reading this very book when, as always suddenly and without forewarning, I was told to turn my face to the wall.

Like, I suspect, most Englishmen, I detest arbitrary orders, and respond and work best when in receipt of explanation. This reflex, the Tupamaros and, I suspect, most totalitarian-educated movements will never understand. I well remember my first photograph, taken on a polar-bear rug at the age of three, with a crisp expatriate-Prussian voice ordering me to 'Laugh, Geoffries!' With just about as much enthusiasm therefore I responded some minutes later to the further instruction to turn round and remove my Afrika Korps skiing cap – veil, padded ear-caps and all – to see what fortune had brought me as my first chance of communication with the outside world, with my family, my government, the roots of all my faith – with all indeed I loved and existed for.

The contemporary press transcriptions of this episode* omit its preamble, and legitimately so. For it began with an apology of its sort, however truculent its presentation.

Unlike my previous quarters my new setting had an element of depth; I never quite knew how many people were about to emerge from its hidden dimensions. So, when obediently I removed my reluctant crash-helmet, I was astonished to find at least three Ku-Klux-Klan-hooded Tupamaros in my small living-space. One was crouched at the head of my truckle-bed, with an up-to-date miniaturized tape-recorder on his lap, and in his hand a microphone poised in the all too familiar 'What-Does-It-Feel-Like?' posture, at the ready and set to go.

* See Appendix 1 for text of interview.

The apology, or explanation, came courteously enough from the random factor in this new equation. It consisted of, so far as I could judge, a young or youngish man. He was enveloped far more copiously than any of my guards, to the extent that the to me by now indifferent grotesquerie of the customary cowl or hood was elaborated to an almost pharaonic extent, with a mask of tight bandages and, unique among all my visitors, a pair of white gloves of the kind to which I would never, in my own philosophy and time, subject even a hired waiter at my table – I wondered and still often wonder what on his hands he had to hide.

He was not, he explained, the visiting correspondent of a major British newspaper whom I had been led to expect. He realized that it must be a disappointment to me not to be speaking to a compatriot, but the misunderstanding had not been intentional, either on his part or that of my captors. However, he would make of our meeting an article which would receive world-wide distribution and, he fully expected, be broadcast over the BBC.

I was not in the least surprised by this disclosure. To be transposed into the 'clandestinity' a writer would need to enjoy the confidence of my captors, preferably indeed to the extent of being committed to them, or vice versa. Equally he would have to expect subsequent exposure to the anathema of the Uruguayan Government for participation in an illegal contact with the urban guerrillas, an unlikely prospect in the case of a reputable British journalist functioning in that part of the world. So I had to decide very quickly whether to contract out of the risk of possible misinterpretation by a biased or even hostile interpreter, or to grasp it as at any rate one means of communication of a sort with the outside world and, hopefully, if the substance and presentation of the interview proved satisfactory, as a means of comfort to my wife and family, and of reassurance to my government. Remembering the all too appropriate proverb of my Near Eastern days – 'The man who doesn't speak, they bury him alive' – I did not hesitate.

Even so, I took my time, and my precautions, with my visitor.

I could not, I said, let down my government by making my first contact with them through one who was not an established pressman of international standing and accreditation. Given existing misunderstandings, could he identify himself by, for example, a press-card? He regretted that for security reasons it was not possible for him to do so. I stated therefore that I would accept him at – so to speak – face-value on the basis of his solemn undertaking, endorsed by my gaolers in the name, and on the honour, of their movement. It is at this point that different versions of this interview which I was to see only after my liberation ostensibly begin. I knew and know nothing of its author. His name – 'Madruga', meaning 'Dawn' in English – could well be a stylized pseudonym of the type frequently affected by Marxist-Leninists, since Stalin and earlier. From his eyes I should have said he was a Central American. They had a certain opacity of which I had learned there to be wary, as if the man of Indian blood, when under stress, anger or fear, draws some kind of a nictating membrane across his normally most expressive eyes. His eventual article bore a Cuban byline, and appeared at the very beginning of April within, I should say, a couple of weeks of its recording.

In his interview Leopaldo Madruga followed for the most part pointedly correct procedures though, even during his first 'warm-up' questions, his alignment if not indeed identification with my captors was evident. He enquired about my material conditions, gradually narrowing down his questions to conditions in the subcontinent and, specifically, in Uruguay, which I declared that I could not as Ambassador debate with him. It seemed to me that his prime hope was to elicit from me some condemnation of the Uruguayan Government, and some endorsement of the Tupamaros above and beyond the purely personal and human capacity to which I insisted on restricting myself. Once or twice anger got the better of him. None of the various transcripts indicates a certain hectoring tone, when he accused me of refusing to talk politics yet, he claimed, introducing them myself by asserting that diplomatic kidnappings were but a fashion like the mini-skirt; there is of course all the difference in the world between the expression of political judgements on a host government's internal politics and political generalization of an abstract and world-wide nature. Furthermore, though I suspect sincerely appreciative of my attempts to inject some humour into an intrinsically lugubrious situation, I do not think that he always wholly grasped them – in for example my querying whether a rescue attempt by the security forces was the most expedient method of seeking my release! It has also struck me as significant that the Montevideo version of the interview omitted my suggestion that the average Tupamaro might grow out of youth's time-honoured reluctance to study that which does not fit its current pattern of beliefs.

The essence of this interview was however that it fulfilled my forecast to my captors that it would deal with them warts and all, and that I would apportion credit and blame impartially. And it is to their credit, and to that of my interviewer, that this impartiality was not interfered with, nor expunged by editing. Nor did its author edit-out his own ideological bias. If perhaps the transcripts do not convey a certain inquisitorial tone which was the interview's most unwelcome aspect to me, I have concluded since my return to normality that such a tone has anyhow lately become the prerogative of the political interviewer, of whatever ideology. For myself, and particularly when witnessing the forensic attitudes often adopted on our own eminently pluralist television towards well-mannered, and well-intentioned, elder statesmen, memory likens them with regret and disapprobation to my own 'interrogation' in a communist cell.

From many books which I have read, and plays I have seen, I have had an idea of the pressure of interrogation. Yet no account, description or representation can communicate the depth of weariness and nervous and physical exhaustion with which so strange an experience leaves its participant. To this sense almost of inward haemorrhage many factors contribute – the dim yellow light which the retina only classifies as such after the occasional intrusion of a floodlight or a photoflash; the bustle and thrust of brisk and impersonal intruders; the strange schizophrenic regret with which one witnesses the departure of one for whom one does not care at all yet who, by an effort of imagination, could be a connecting-cord with all those for whom one does truly care. I recall too the acute and disproportionate anxiety, the childish fear of deprival, with which I noticed that some physical inconvenience to the gathering was created by the tilt at the head of my flock mattress; I had achieved it by contriving to retain my shoes, in my first gaol confiscated from me but returned for the transfer. Strategically wedged, they held up my head, to relieve my by now quite sore shoulders; also, from time to time, I could put my hand under the mattress, and actually touch a sole that had stood on my own carpet, with my wife and my son, and the velvet of a suède that had first caught my eye in a London shop, which still no doubt held English dust, and which I was insistently determined would once again walk a London street with my wife.

So it has; and all the length of the toe-cap there still runs the faint crease where the shoes folded flat under the weight of my mattress and my head. But, though I keep these shoes, to see and to remember, and at the time dreaded their removal, I do not care to wear them any more.

Chapter 14

M y visitor had come and gone without a face. Within a few days I was to see one more face, with a single special exception the only other human countenance I was to be allowed to see till I returned to mankind. For once, in this underworld, I found myself at the viewing rather than the participating end when another human being was thrust, dumped like some kind of a package, appalled, horrified yet unvanquished, into this abominable environment.

Quite exceptionally it happened without the usual advance ritual of my being hooded and told to turn to the wall. There was simply the sound of harsh voices and urgent feet; the curtain outside the little communal 'lobby' to cells No 9 and No 10 was opened, and, next, the door to No. 9 at right angles to my own. Down the corridor was propelled a tall and strongly built man whom two hooded young men spun on his heels and projected through the door. Without a word they slammed it behind him and, as with myself earlier, proceeded to insert padlocks through the hasps of the heavy bolts, with much parade of heavily charged key-rings.

I have seldom seen a man so deliberately compose himself and bring himself under control. His whole frame was vibrating with nervous shock; that this reaction was anything but the trembling of fear was in any case at once evident from his first response. 'Good day,' I said. 'I know you, Ambassador,' he replied, 'and you know my family although you don't know me. My name is Ferrés, Ricardo Ferrés, a rather broken-up Uruguayan whom these strange compatriots of mine – for whose behaviour to you I apologize – have brought here for no useful reason that I can see.' I smiled, and said 'If I could offer you my hand I would'; for the heavy wire mesh between our cages would hardly let a finger or two through, though later our gaolers cut a kind of letter-box in it so that we could pass each other our books. Thanks to it I was literally able to extend to Ricardo a helping hand when, later and inevitably as had I in my own time too, he also had to pass through his own dark night of the soul. But from the first moment I knew that here was a man whom nothing would shatter. He will not I know resent my elaborating on his self-introduction, since it is a matter of history that, although a brilliant industrialist, in his banking capacity he had just gone spectacularly bankrupt, largely – I surmise – as a result of economic and market forces beyond his own local control. Later I was able to tell his captors that I found ironic their making an ideological example of the one man – at that a man whose skills and integrity I was able to watch them increasingly respect for themselves – who so patently demonstrated the risk-factor in capitalism rather than its exploitational aspect for their ideology.

But this was not yet the time to engage in such a disputation. Not only was there a guard perched on a stool in the corner between our two cells – from this time on such a fixture was never to be absent – but instantly another young man irrupted to address himself to Señor Ferrés. I do not believe that his exempting me from the ensuing diatribe was due to any regard for my immunities or tenure, but simply that subjection to instant reflex, excessive weaponry and total ferocity was expected to impress a new captive more than myself. It was the old familiar psychological warfare; and I was delighted and impressed to see that, though Ricardo Ferrés took his cue from it, he was even so early in the proceedings neither intimidated nor fooled by it.

The essence of the warning was that same against which I myself had been compelled to fight a steady though not so difficult rearguard action during my brief companionship with Señor Berro – that only perfunctory conversation would be allowed. The difference now was that they were dealing with a total newcomer, not one who had already spent weeks and months in the underworld. They also believed that they would be able to impress him by overt threats of violence, and occult references to their omniscience and omnipotence. The threat was that a recalcitrant prisoner exposed himself to physical disciplines culminating, if necessary, in 'execution' – a term incidentally which I have never accepted as valid coinage, since it implies both a crime and a judgement, neither of which is legitimately applicable in such circumstances. The implication was that 'we have ways of knowing'. It meant in practice that not only were prisoners virtually permanently invigilated by a standing, or more literally, seated guard, but that supplementary vigilance irrupted in the form of spot-checks. For these the guard was spuriously withdrawn for brief periods, during which a careful observer could identify visual and auditory monitoring, i.e. lurking shadows and whispers, behind the plastic screens surrounding the two cells. This is not to underestimate the sophistication of my captors' electronic monitoring devices, which I discovered extended not merely to a permanent microphone/amplifier/loudspeaker system, culminating in a kind of studio at another end of the 'barracks', but even to a permanently functioning tape-recorder, recording not merely surreptitious comments to or from my neighbour but even my snores and sleep-talking for my insatiably curious hosts' archives.

But a captive has his own curiosity, as one means of whiling the days away, as well as a strong competitive urge to locate even the most insignificant chinks in his captors' apparent invulnerability. So my neighbour and I had the at least internal satisfaction of cutting this turnkey officiousness and bullyragging down to size, by gradually identifying its pedestrian nature. Visually it consisted of simple peeping as, on one occasion, a simple trick of light and shade gave away; and, auditively, of strategically placed microphones, easily located and, I hope, once or twice accidentally blasted by a convenient sneeze. Of their nonstop functioning I have no doubt; on more than one occasion I found myself able to summon my captors, by experimenting on the analogy of a similar technological device commonly marketed as the electronic baby-sitter.

Nonetheless, though the implementation of our surveillance

had its lapses, there was a serious moral to be learned from the dressing-down administered to my neighbour, by a youth less than half his age – less indeed than that of his own son who died tragically and unreported to him during his father's captivity. The lesson, it seemed to me then, and seems increasingly as time passes, was that of the essential ferocity of our captors. Force differs from violence, not only by measurable degree but in moral quality; and raw violence, whether implemented for personal or political gain, for lucrative or for ideological purposes, cannot simply be switched on by human beings without the added forced-draught of naked ferocity. The castigation of my neighbour counts as one of those periodic reminders of a personal experience to which forgetfulness, whatever the extent of forgiveness, may never with honesty be applied. I have therefore concluded, not least with the help of the reminder which I have described, that ferocity, far more than precise ideology, was the main single and common component of my captors' assorted personalities. Where it had not existed, or had been only latent, it had to be learned, or to emerge, for its host to live in consistency with himself.

That ferocity, active or latent, with which for so long I lived, represented I found one of the most exhausting pressures against which the subconscious mind had to stand fast. I hope that, in singling out this isolated flurry of which my fellow captive was victim, I have not appeared inconsistent with my acknowledgement of individual acts of compassion or fairness. I cannot but recall, in wondering at this paradox, a great Canadian doctor's assertion to me that one person out of nine in today's streets, as against the one in thirty of his student days, will spend part of their life in some sort of a mental institution. All political considerations and aspirations apart, could it be that the violence, the ferocity, of clandestinity have no intellectual let alone ethical component, but instead are just another symptom of a deranged body-chemistry, just another mechanistic function of mankind's alienation from a world and a society with which he is ever more incompatible?

I myself am all too capable of great anger; but I believe, and hope, that the human explosion which I saw that day, and on other days, was something else. Such ferocity is in itself something else, something animal-plus. The animal's is an innocent ferocity, while that of man contains hate, or madness. If the extra factor is hate, then it is comprehensible that man should be termed the only animal that can sin. If it is madness, then it may well be true that the practitioners of the new violence are, to a man and to a woman, just sick, however dangerously so to themselves and to their fellow men.

Whether sick or sane our hosts, the presence of a neighbour was a solace to me, as I hope mine was to him.

Chapter 15

By some synergical effect the acquisition of a neighbour in the adjoining cell did more than just double the social dimension of my life. As a virtual hermit I had been scrutinized, visited, inspected only. With two of us it now seemed to me that our guards were really 'doing their rounds', and that life had taken a pattern. Perhaps too society as an institution stimulates the formation of salutary routines as solitude does not. By extension then civilization would be the function and product of societies rather than of accumulated solitudes. I certainly had in my own time of solitude set up my own routines. But they had been an effort; and with a neighbour they became easier to pursue and much wider in their scope.

Whether it is an original discovery or not I cannot say; but I have concluded that the captive requires two classes of routine, corresponding to two distinct human needs – the need to break up his day, and the need to fill up his day. I had already developed many such routines and, with company, was to develop more.

In retrospect I can rationalize what at the time I suspect I did intuitively to survive, which was to confront the loss of the dimension of time – and the effective extinction of any future tense – by the creation of landmarks in my small eternity. Just as the traveller in a snowstorm survives the mortal danger of wandering in a circle by taking even the shortest of bearings from one visible tree to the next, so the captive must break up his 'day' into stages from one to the other of which he can progress without vertigo, emotional, intellectual, even spiritual. In my case the stages were of the simplest, furnishing something to look forward to, and a space to fill up profitably meanwhile.

For this reason meals become very important to a captive.

Plain hunger is their secondary aspect; only once or twice did I experience it, and then never by the intention of my captors. Far more significant is their function as a compass bearing in a wilderness of time. Many writers have left us with harrowing vignettes of captives circling or crouched at the bottom of their pit or oubliette, awaiting with almost languorous entreatment the flung crust or hambone. Far more than from the pain of an empty belly, their anguish sprang, I can vouch, from the fear of an empty mind and an empty space of time.

So I admit, ruefully but without shame, that I was usually awake in time and waiting to see the guard stir on his chair, for the hum of the small overnight fan to be swamped by the cough, falter and roar of the great air-turbine of daytime activity and, soon, for that first so welcome glass of tea, preceded by the smoothly bitten half-apple – or half-dozen slices of orange depending on the season of the year outside – cleanly and carefully hoarded overnight in the hygiene of an equally carefully preserved plastic bag.

Some hours later, at what I considered my lunchtime, an adequate ample meal would normally be served. I would try to leave on one side, untouched, the carbohydrate component; when the young are about nothing edible is ever wasted! The fruit I would try to divide, or hoard, so that I should have some left over to balance my last meal of the day, and for my 'breakfast' next day. The last meal, as always, comprised what had not been served hot of the midday meal, served cold before sleeping. Between the two was a long and belly-aching stretch, alleviated however by a tea-time of sorts.

I had told my journalistic interviewer of some weeks before that tea had acquired almost a mystic significance in my existence, partly because of its symbolism of a happier reality, and partly because it was a cup of tea which had first allowed me to see one of my captors laugh. When first thrust my 'morning tea' I was so elated that I burst quite spontaneously if unmelodiously into song. When my gaoler asked me what I was singing in English, I replied with an impromptu Spanish rendering – of which in retrospect I am by no means ashamed – of 'I Like a Nice Cup of Tea', to the vast amusement of, by this time, my assembled guards. I came back to England just in time to be able to pass the message to the original's author, the late Sir Alan Herbert, that 'he had done it again', and had produced laughter where before there had only been anxiety and gloom. In two other ways his recent autobiography had helped me – by the straight-faced but useful physiotherapy of his 'Rolling the Abdominal Wall', and by the childlike candour of his replacement, as a First World War subaltern needful of sleep, of sheep-counting by the rhythmic repetition of the phrase 'Thank God – Don't be afraid.' With the one I was able to replace unavailable exercise space, and with the other unwelcome soporifics.

I usually tried to do my first bout of exercises – not too long a one – immediately before my 'breakfast'. By this time I had wandered quite far from their original Candian framework, partly because, where 'my first floor had finished by not being clean enough to lie on, the new floor simply was not big enough. In addition the circumstances of confinement had produced a certain physical change in an old enemy of mine, a chest-hernia acquired when rowing as a student, which suddenly made press-ups and such-like horizontal exercises painful and possibly risky. So I devised alternatives and, in particular, adhered to and developed my running-on-the-spot and skipping, to an extent that each day, in assorted shifts, I 'jogged' the equivalent of not less, and usually far more, than five miles.

After a reasonably strenuous instalment of exercise, and a tea-bag perhaps stretched out into two cups, I was always pleasantly ready for what, after the long deprivation of my first dungeon, had become my greatest luxury – my 'ablutions'. Here there was no lack of cold water; and I never lost what must be akin to the joy and reverence of a beduin or a Tuareg for my two-gallon plastic *bidon* of cold, sweet water. Whether to drink or to keep my body clean, it was no longer a convenience or a convention but so dire a necessity that it had become, and remains, a luxury and a delight. About once a fortnight my gaolers would produce hot water and soap for me to wash my hair and beard. One day however my current gaoler announced that the 'familia' had received an electric shaver with which I might now remove this never very welcome growth. After the briefest of experiments with it I was able to tell him that external and prior assistance would be indispensable; so he came – rather cautiously – into my cell with what I considered an unnecessarily blunt pair of scissors. Despite some tweaking and the occasional minor accident, he performed an adequate task of preliminary clearing, after which I was allowed to proceed for myself to the definitive operation of a true shave. The whole procedure seemed to me an updated and electrified version of a scene remembered from so many child-hood films – the Western in which the cow-hand or prospector 'comes into town' after a long and unhygienic absence, to luxuriate in his first bath and the removal of his beard. In my case I deter-mined never to allow matters to degenerate so far again, at least so long as the equipment was available, and from then on con-trived to shave daily, to the great good of my morale. At the back of my mind was also, I believe, the determination to emerge from my captivity, if I were to do so, with such dignity as was possible, rather than as an object of curiosity or even pity.

A little later my improvised barber volunteered to cut my hair also if I was prepared to risk it. He was in fact, or so he maintained, a hairdresser. I asked him if by this assertion he was referring to some honorary, volunteer or even part-time capacity merely related to his function in the barracks and on my guard-roster. His reply – that he was semi-professional – was quite revealing of the formation, background and motivation of his movement and of its membership and recruitment. I happened to have gathered earlier that he had been a university student before taking to the clandestine existence. He went on to explain that he had been a practising spare-time hairdresser in order to eke out his earnings when doing a vacation job on a succession of cattle-estancias, and had continued at it in a 'moon-lighting' capacity during term-time. So I need not be alarmed about his competence. I replied acknowledging it, but pointing out that conversely I was in no position to pay either the recognized professional tariff, or percentage!

In the event, I decided to hedge my bet, and asked him to give me the simplest of basin-crops, from which I painfully concluded that his status was still largely amateur. However, the operation sufficed to keep him at bay till his tour of duty was over, and I was safe from his well-intentioned solicitude. I was to survive on this one haircut till my release, rightly gambling that with time the already perceptible advance of the longer-haired fashion would spread from young to middle-aged males, even if only in an attenuated degree. So the months of my incarceration found yet another positive aim. With an element of more truth than flippancy I have occasionally been able to answer the question as to how I passed my time by alleging that I just sat there growing my hair.

Another milestone in the days, a mysterious one and therefore a strangely unpleasant routine, unlike the wholesome cold-water ablutions which it regularly followed, was a daily ceremony entitled 'la ventilación'. Just what was being ventilated I never knew; my cell was quite adequately ventilated, apart from the massive air-duct system feeding the air-supply of the barracks installation as a whole, by a small supplementary turbine behind the wire of my exercise-alcove, at floor level. Only when, very occasionally, this machine broke down or blew a fuse, did my quarters become stuffy or over-heated, in great contrast to the authentic and permanent Black Hole of Calcutta setting of my first People's Prison.

I have often therefore wondered if this recurrent drill was not something more than a simple and apparently unnecessary stirring of the abundant dust of my premises from one place to another. On the call 'Ventilación!' we were trained, like a laboratory animal taught now to do for itself what at first was done to it, to take down from a nail the Afrika Korps or ski-cap-style headgear to which I have already referred, and which at first had been brusquely jammed over our heads for us on occasions when we were required to be incommunicado. They were a version –

locally made 'import-substitute' I imagine – of the type of cheap plastic peaked cap, with ear-flaps, like a latterday and not very attractive kepi, used often by young men on motor-bicycles and scooters in the less temperate parts and seasons of Europe. The ear-flaps had however been heavily padded with a hard wadding of compressed cotton wool, and a cloth veil stitched under the peak. When therefore the strap of the ear-flaps was pulled tight, with the veil under one's chin, both sight and sound were excluded. Even so, we were instructed to keep our face to the wall, in that all too accustomed posture, while I hauled up my blanket and hunched my shoulders against a chill blast of unknown mechanical origin.

The ritual lasted for quite some time, and part of it, from the background of sound, was straightforward house-work; I could hear the duckboards lifted and dropped – these had been *de rigueur*, even in my new and more salubrious surroundings, since our first establishment had been swamped by sewage during the first torrents of the rainy season. But I also noticed that other operations seemed to be synchronized with it. Not only was this the time when, quite naturally, the process of dusting appeared invariably to have reshuffled the familiar and careful order of my gradually swelling library; this after all is a phenomenon which can occur within the privacy and canon of a man's home. The difference is when papers, things written, are out of order, or even have gone away. So, rightly or wrongly, I always identified the routine of 'ventilación' as primarily some form of inspection and censorship. Whatever its purpose, I found it a vexation and, obscurely, a humiliation.

Very often I would while away the 'ventilación' by taking a catnap, an aptitude which, over the years, I have made a conscious effort to acquire. I know of no more effective adjunct to exercise – as defined for the middle-aged man and as striven for, within the limitations of a dungeon setting, by myself over those long months – than the process of getting healthily tired but never exhausted. So often I had found in ordinary life, in what I came to think of as real life, that ten minutes' sound sleep could set back the frontier of fatigue, leaving me to face a function or assignment without exhaustion. This discipline was to prove invaluable, and indeed a great comfort, in captivity.

For in general I slept well, and could look forward to the end of my 'day' with equanimity. Still more, I could break it in two by a siesta of sorts, which strengthened and rested me for yet more exercise, provided a further respite of withdrawal into the blessed refuge of sleep, and broke up the day with yet another of those landmarks to which I could look forward. So it was that I discovered the wisdom of installing in my waking day these successive compartments, between which there extended portions of time which it was my next duty to fill as wisely and profitably as I could.

PART FOUR

MIND, MEN AND WOMEN

Chapter 16

As appetite is alleged to grow with eating, perhaps total recall is stimulated by the effort of remembering. Certainly the process of disinterring from the accumulating rubble of memory those already and all too eagerly buried boundary-marks and milestones with which I set out my days has brought back much of the detail with which I filled out their consecutive spaces. From nowhere, yet with disconcerting clarity, I recall one of my custodians, a stalwart and rather dour young man, asking me if I had finished yet some particular project of which we had spoken. I replied no; that for a couple of days I expected to be far too busy to have time for it. I recall his halting, turning, the expression of his eyes through his mask and, finally, his short laugh – 'Time is the one thing I should have thought you had more than enough of.'

I myself had to laugh at the irony of what I had said so solemnly. Again my mind returned to the long days of that one remote childhood sickness. I saw myself each day rearranging my small effects, making a little desk out of my books and magazines – a kind of Carlton House desk, with its gallery and sloping walls for privacy. I heard myself too, insisting to myself even then how busy I was, reassuring myself how much remained for me to do. And here I was, fifty years on, earnestly convincing myself, in just the same way, how busy I still was keeping myself. In the psychology of captivity, perhaps one of the greatest of therapies could be this capacity to put on again childish things, or at the least a childish approach towards serious things.

For their substance – especially that of my reading-matter – was all too far from being childish. The urban guerrilla is encouraged to be extremely serious-minded; reading and indoctrination are intended to be effectively synonymous in his case. For the whole of my three or so months in my first dungeon I depended entirely on their mildewed and well-thumbed field-library, with one or two specific and monumental exceptions; and how repetitive, turgid and dull it was – save as a technical exercise – to one who did not share but was totally repelled by its ethic and orientation. But I have promised myself that these present recollections shall not be tarnished or vitiated by ideological and polemical attitudes. So I will make no comment on the content of my captors' collection of the works of Che Guevara, Regis Debray, Menuhim Begin, and so many other authorities produced after some weeks, possibly for my edification, certainly to while away my time, equally certainly not for my entertainment. I will not deny that when the serial version of Tolstoy's *Anna Karenina* started reaching me, instalment by instalment, I thanked God. Its closing description of Levine, seeking as ever to find some transcendental purpose out of the majesty of the physical universe, was good fare for a man who was beginning to forget the aspect of the night sky, let alone the daylight world.

The first book I received was a Bible; my captors had taken good note of my daily habits, and I shall always give them full credit for this first conclusion they drew from them. It is however my intention, if my courage does not fail me, to seek to bring together separately, elsewhere than in these recollections, the strange and irrefutable responses of the human spirit to captivity and solitude. In that less cerebral setting my Bible, or rather its successive manifestations, should find its rightful place, as against the present account of my more secular library.

It became self-evident that some sort of clearance had been given at policy level that I should now be allowed to read; not only did *Anna Karenina* appear spontaneously but I was even asked what, in reason, I would like thereafter. I had already realized with prison fare, whether edible or intellectual, that bulk, solidity and staying-power are prime virtues. So without hesitation I indented for Cervantes, or Shakespeare, or both. For the time I had to be content with *Don Quijote*, which more than fulfilled its purpose and my hopes; I read it over and over again, viewing it from different angles – literary, linguistic, historical, even economic and social. Yet as time went by, and for the first time in almost a lifetime's familiarity, I found myself disturbed in the *Quijote* by a sadness, an indifference if not callousness oscillating between passive fatalism and active cruelty, the discernment or imagining of which I can only attribute to a subjective reaction to my own circumstances at the time. Perhaps we need to be set back from situations of pain far enough to be able to discern the degree of compassion intended in their viewing. The fact remains, when a further copy of the *Quijote* was produced for me after my translation to my second hideaway, I found myself returning to it less and less.

It was in my second dungeon that the flow of literature really grew. I formed the conclusion that my captors had two main sources in the outside world – the open market, and private libraries with more than a suggestion of the school-prize collection to them. Neither is improbable. Montevideo has a substantial industry revolving round the purchase, sale and exchange of second-hand books, mainly paperbacks. These began to appear in large quantities, frequently with no effort to hide their provenance, the rubber-stamped mark of the vendor being familiar to me in many cases. For the most part, at first, these books were in Spanish, and were intended for my guards; I had the impression that those responsible for policy had concluded that, however desirable in theory, man cannot live underground on an exclusive intellectual diet of indoctrination and propaganda. Increasingly therefore the entertainment and pabulum function showed in the selection; my guards passed them on to me, and I enjoyed them.

Even more however were things looking up when the second, and I assume private source of reading-matter began to come my way. To begin with, another policy-decision, for me of quantum-jump dimensions, determined that I should be allowed books in my own language. I rejoiced in it, though not for reasons of linguistic convenience; had I not already done so anyhow, by this time I would have been reading Spanish like English. Its major and most marvellous effect was immensely to widen the scope and content of what I was reading. One after another now there reached me those well-bound presentation classics, on fine paper and with the flyleaf rigorously removed along with all incriminating evidence of origin and ownership. In the first consignment were the complete works of Shakespeare at last, the collected essays of Aldous Huxley, and the collected works of Oscar Wilde. The last, as with Cervantes, I found myself reading with diminishing enjoyment. With Wilde redemption seemed to me too closely blended with despair, whether the protagonist was Dorian Gray or the poor murderer of Reading Gaol. In any event, Wilde's not unreasonable final obsession with prison-bars was too near the bone for me; in one of his letters from Reading Gaol he describes the torment of a plank-bed, on a fair specimen of which I was making my best and not wholly unsuccessful endeavours to find some comfort at the very time of reading.

Huxley and Shakespeare shared a particular merit for me, though only Shakespeare has that quality of the infinitely applicable raw material, of the built-in Philosopher's Stone, which makes him self-transmutable and instantly available for whatever purpose of the human heart and mind; thus I was even able to work out army-letter-type pro-forma messages to my wife, by which a single reference, comprising a whole scene or sonnet – Number Twenty-seven for example – would serve for an economy-code if ever I were to be permitted to write to her. But both writers, with their quality of the polymath, brought with them that amplifying capacity which I have mentioned, and which like some kind of wide-angle lens infinitely broadened the horizons of my some few cubic yards of subterranean cell. If I never suffered from claustrophobia – and I feared far more than the physical its mental and intellectual variant – the merit goes to these two writers, with their capacity to swing their reader around and about in time, space, and intellectual discipline.

A further quantum-jump in the life of my mind was to be prompted by the academic background and presumable accomplishments of many of my captors, and their ensuant access to

large, grave and sustaining volumes of honorific and com-
memorative aspect. Having accustomed themselves to the idea
of my receiving English books, they noticed that I showed
familiarity with other languages. French, German, Italian, all
appeared in their turn; I even found myself brushing up some by
now almost non-existent ancient Greek. A particular help in this
latter process was derived from my captors' delivering one day a
large and expensively presented – though, I noticed, most
diminutively priced – copy of the *Soviet Encyclopedia of Philosophy*
which, whatever its current biographical or historical omissions,
was commendably complete in its translation into Greek of
standard philosophical terms. From it I drew my refresher-
course, and also re-learned to write in Greek characters.

In French a book which gave me particular joy was a biography
of the Czech-German poet Rainer Maria Rilke, not least for its
'two-for-the-price-of-one' quality, most of the copious quota-
tions being in the original German. Rilke has always seemed to
me a particularly interesting poet, having traits that extend from
a fin-de-siècle, Art Nouveau, Beardsley connotation up to the
'Art Déco' and even to the early Existentialist vein of the twenties.
More especially, I have always simply liked his verse; and it was
with a particular pleasure, even poignancy, that I was able to re-
read in captivity his beautiful poem, 'The Panther'. I have
wondered since how many captives besides myself, and in how
many prison, war, death, concentration-camps, have comforted
themselves with this magnificent image of the caged beast, pad-
ding round and around behind his bars till, in the end, it is he who
is still, whose eyes stare unblinking from some vast pivot of force,
out onto a world of prison-bars that is spinning around him. By
some curious extension of thought, this inversion of the captive's
role by a great poet gave me much comfort, and the certainty
that, in the midst of madness and fury, it was I who remained
calm and sane.

My two main German standbys were both of the 'bought-by-
the-pound' – if not by-the-yard – variety. It is only since my
time as a prisoner that I have fully appreciated the Victorian taste

for novels of massive substance; I doubt if ever again I shall
seriously rate a book as a proper book – even my own – at less
than eight hundred pages clear. For this, though for individually
discrete reasons also, I appreciated equally well Jochem Klepper's
Der Vater and Thomas Mann's *Zauberberg*. The first, 'The Father',
recounts the upbringing of Frederick the Great of Prussia by a
father pathologically determined to fit him for greatness. Its
great merit to me was its close grain and stylistic beauty, which
I could chew and savour slowly like a wholesome rye-bread. At
a time when sleep was beginning to be something of a problem
for me I could rely on this book to comfort my wakefulness, or to
court elusive sleep, with equal facility and even with something
remotely approaching happiness. For to the captive comparisons
are not always or necessarily odious; even misery can count its
relative blessings. So I am grateful to Klepper, whose bright future
was terminated by his own hand in 1942 – to save his Jewish wife
and half-Jewish child from Himmler – for having reminded me,
from familiar history, of the physical and emotional wretchedness
so senselessly endured by a good father for a great son, and vice
versa. In my darkness I prayed for Klepper's soul, as I clung to
mine.

I cannot be so sententious about my affection for 'The Magic
Mountain', a book which on all previous readings I had found
intolerable. Not so this time round, and not simply because I was
thankful for small mercies, even disguised as long books. I had
never much cared for the allegorical aspect of Mann's depiction
of the hothouse life of a pre-World War One tuberculosis
sanatorium, rudely disrupted by the implacable whirlwind of
war. Now I found it curiously intriguing, the reason being, I
suppose, that his hero too, though a hypochondriac and an eager
volunteer for the cosseted and selective monasticism of sanatorium
life, was living like myself a life apart in a totally enclosed society.
Inside it Mann's characters too found it necessary, or desirable, to
evolve their own rituals and disciplines. So there was much to
compare, and a salutary possibility to identify and guard against
signs of morbidity caused by introversion and self-obsession.

In fact, my greatest single source of affection for an otherwise not particularly – I find – endearing book came from my having struck gold in it in the form of an entirely new game of solitaire. Minutest description is a characteristic of Mann's technique, whether of settings, conversations or actions – hence his to me, at the time, most meritorious attribute, which I hope I may now be forgiven for describing as sesquipedalian prolixity; to me anything approaching a thousand pages flat was then a blessing, and not even in disguise. So three full pages delineating every aspect of an entirely unknown game of patience was a true mother-lode; and I exploited it to the last ounce. It was known as 'The Solitaire of Thirteen' and, since my return home, I have vainly looked for it in assorted books of patiences, though my courage has not extended to trudging again, for that reason alone, through several hundred pages of the *Zauberberg*. Even so, and although by some strange memory-block I cannot at this moment reconstitute what was in essence the simplest of card-games, I was thankful for it at the time, as I was for the book itself which, read soberly and painstakingly, could guarantee me, each time over, several days of effective escape from my cell.

Escape was particularly needed for some of my more forbidding Spanish-language reading, though in fact the finest escape route of all came in the end from Spanish translations of a famous compatriot who shall have the most honourable of recognitions. But for a long, long time much of my Spanish-language literature, in original or translation, was heavily doctrinaire or tendentious. My captors had for example a particular affection for protest-literature of all kinds. Franz Fanon, with his *Wretched of the Earth* and its presentation, if not indeed justification, of the pathology of violence, was one favourite. So too were the works of the American Negro intellectuals and Black Panthers; I particularly recall the constantly adduced writings of Rap Brown and James Baldwin, neither of whom seemed to me to justify any contention that their intelligence and talents had been stunted by their particular societies. Latin American fiction included the novels of García Márquez; I have described how I was reluctantly photographed with his *Cien Años de Soledad* – too good a novel to be conscripted as mere visual propaganda. I was also given *La Ciudad y Los Perros*, by the Peruvian Vargas Llosa, strangely translated into English, I now see, as 'Time of the Heroes'; *La Tregua* – 'The Truce' – of the Uruguayan Mario Benedetti; *Los Pasos Perdidos* – 'The Lost Steps' – of the Cuban Alejandro Carpentier; *La Inondación* – 'The Flood' – of the Argentine Sylvia Bulrich.

These, and many more, were from much the same cloth – brilliantly written, but sad, pessimistic, even morbid and decomposing. They brought little light into my life or joy to my heart, any more than, for other reasons, I was able to work up a sincere enthusiasm at the time for *Papillon*, by the French author Henri Charrière, best-seller as deservedly it was; it was offered to me with some misgivings by one of my gaolers, who doubted whether a book detailing alternating imprisonment in and escapes from Devil's Island was recommended reading for one in my position. On sampling I was inclined to agree with him, and decided to finish it some other time, which has not yet arrived.

By now it will be clear that such catch-phrases as 'escape-literature' and 'escapism' acquire in captivity a very different and more literal reality. 'To Althea, From Prison' joins with many other such latent if unsuspected memories in a new and more pointed significance; though longing for the wings of a dove, the captive also learns to identify and benefit from those aspects of his new life in which stone walls do truly not a prison make, nor the all too solid iron bars a cage. Imagination, and – even in a dungeon – mirth, can in their fashion melt the bars away; the second time I laughed at my own bars was thanks to a boyhood recollection of Mr. Stanley Holloway's famous lion Wallace, when I awoke on my floor and realized that I too was 'in a somnolent posture, with the side of my head on the bars'.

But my truest escapism was achieved the day when one of my gaolers enquired if I could tell him anything of a compatriot of mine of whom they had received some books – her name was 'Agata Creestee'. From that moment I never lacked an escape-route back to my native land, an escape-route of far greater and more instant efficacity than the 'space-warp' beloved of science-fiction writers. With the help of Dame Agatha, and a small effort of will, the infinite separation of the galaxies was instantly bridged, the opposed dimensions of captivity and freedom were brought together at their time-gate, the propositions of Einstein and the Laws of Thermodynamics – with all but a few spatial and temporal formalities – effectively bypassed.

To the subjective joy of so improbable a time-journeying could be added a particular intellectual bonus – the spectacle of young revolutionaries, drenched in a relativist view of society, drawn towards two such implacable defenders of moral absolutes as Miss Marples and Monsieur Poirot. In intellectual discussion my hosts unfailingly revealed themselves as total pragmatists; politically and tactically their yardstick was unvaryingly 'Does it work?' Yet here they were, betraying an ardent nostalgia for the more intransigent criteria of 'Is it right?' and 'Is it wrong?' Miss Marples – as too Monsieur Poirot in his perhaps subtler way – possesses a quality of candour, even of innocence, but combined with a nose for evil which would impel either of them to pursue the scent of murder to the end of its trail with all the tenacity of the bloodhounds of Heaven itself. Yet these characters, symbols of a whole ethic, attracted the unqualified admiration of young terrorists who, nevertheless, could rationalize even murder to their total satisfaction. I did not know whether to weep for their lost innocence, or to pin my hopes on these disarming evidences of its vestigial survival.

Chapter 17

I**T** may seem that the first and shorter part of my captivity was richer in episode, and leaner in reflection, than the second and longer sojourn in the more sophisticated version of my People's Prison. This impression is, I have concluded, only another factor of the 'accordion-effect' I have so often noticed. With the much longer period in my second prison, episodes and happenings were stretched out over a far longer period. Just as within its walls I had developed my own routines, so also my captors were developing their own adaptations to monotony in step with the world outside. During these long months, I was to learn, I was often referred to, in that world without, as 'the forgotten man'. The phrase was well intentioned, and aimed to perpetuate concern for my continuing well-being, and indeed, my physical survival. But it was not necessary. I was never forgotten and, obscurely, I knew it.

What simply was happening was that events, episodes, were spread out, and over much more time, no longer hours, but days, weeks and months. Between the now more widely separated landmarks day-to-day routine rather than adrenalinous confrontation was what filled my days, and my calendar. It was significant that interrogations, even visits, virtually dwindled to nothing, to the extent that more than once I was told to expect an important visit 'next week' and, a month later, it had still not materialized. In any event, my time-killing therapies had meanwhile acquired their own significance and justification.

I had for example made the curious discovery that my 'patiences' were not really patiences at all; after my return home I was able to cross-check this impression against the expertise of my wife, not to mention several standard handbooks. It was quite clear that the three assorted 'solitaires' I had remembered, or evolved, were not at all games-of-chance which I had seen, watched and dredged up from subconscious memory. They were simply pattern-making activities with which – provided I concentrated and made no gross error of memory or judgement – I could not go wrong. I can only assume that their regular rehearsal satisfied my profound need to assure myself constantly that mine was still a universe of order, and of laws, and still to some measure subject to my own free will. Certainly the occasions were many when I withdrew contented into sleep, tired out because I had refused to be satisfied till the symmetry and order had been achieved which I expected my functioning mind to produce from the initial confusion of the random cards.

At an early stage, when I had first been given a pack of cards and had started using them for solitaire, my custodians invited me to play their own card-games with them. They particularly enjoyed playing the classic River Plate card-game of 'truco'. As its name implies, it is a game involving a considerable element of near-cheating, but not of the laconic and, literally, poker-faced kind. Truco is, I suspect, a bar-game, and necessitates much table-thumping, card-slapping and, indeed, laughter; I think I must have seen its ancestor in some of the Arab countries long ago.

I appreciated that this offer to join with me, or to have me join them, came certainly from higher authority, probably from genuine concern for my welfare and, quite possibly, from authentic kindness; it extended incidentally to chess and to draughts also. I felt ungracious refusing it, and gave as a reason what in fact was not a cause but a consequence. I explained that card-games, like chess and checkers, did not affect me as those fortunate people to whom they are a relaxant; and it is in fact true that all these games, instead of restoring me from fatigue, have instead always produced it, and that a game of bridge at the end of a tiring day is for me an additional weariness amounting to a torture.

In my peculiar circumstances I might even so have needed pastimes, and company, badly enough to find these reactions superseded. If I did not, the reason was a psychological one, too powerful for me to unblock, and too irrational for me to admit it to my gaolers. All those time-killing games had to be played with the captive on one side of the wire-grille door, and with the captor on the other. The passing of cards, or the moving of a piece, required the captive to bend down to the little cat-door at the foot of the main door; to kneel; and to put his hand through in order to participate. To me this was no longer a game; I like my competitiveness to deploy itself as between equals and without pre-established moral disadvantages. Even in receiving my food at floor-level I felt an element of abasement; though I believe that, rather than the back-bending, it was the passing of the hand through a chicken-hatch that something within me resented. In any case a gesture essential in order to eat – for survival no less – may honourably be turned down for purposes of simple entertainment.

Perhaps the canons of captivity know no logic for this one particular gesture to have seemed so repugnant to me. For there were other mental and vocal pastimes, eventually shared with my captors, which still presupposed the existence of a physical barrier between us. Yet perhaps it did not count so much if there was no bending, crouching, trap-opening and arm-stretching. I was always, during these long months, on guard against any morbid hypersensitivity; but this was one situation in which I could consciously repudiate the posture of a suppliant. So the same instinctive caveat did not function in my mind where social contacts – party-games, however inappropriate the phrase may seem – could be pursued by talking, but not reaching, through the wire.

The most strenuous of these, and the most revealing of my captors' psychology, was what they called 'Numbers'. It was a game mathematical in form but logical in execution. Each party had a pencil and a paper, and wrote on it a number – his number. His opponent was required to guess it by a process of elimination. At first the number was of four digits, but as we became more expert we progressed to six. One party would announce to his opponent his 'shot' at his opponent's number. The reply might be 'one right; one fair', which meant that he had guessed one right digit in its right place, one digit right but out of place, and two entirely wrong. Luck could intervene as when, for example, the reply was 'four wrong', in which case four of the ten numbers from one to zero could be eliminated, leaving only six to identify and place, with copious use of pencil and paper.

This process of elimination was essentially an exercise in logic; and my guards explained to me that it was specifically recommended and encouraged for those on guard-shift, as a means of preserving mental suppleness and improving their training for subsequent operational activity, by enhancing their powers of concentration and speed of mental reflex.

I admit that I derived more pleasure from the spectator-sport than from the participation, and from studying my captors' techniques and responses rather than improving my own. It interested me that the better performers were invariably among my women guards, one of whom it was who elevated the sport to the three-dimensional chess level of abstraction represented by its six-digit variant; though chess itself seemed to be more an addiction of the menfolk. In all these intellectual games it seemed to me that the men were the more aggressive and emotional, and the women – literally – more calculating, yet in their way, once prepared to 'fraternize with the enemy', more gregarious and spontaneously social.

As such a social activity the playing of music did not count. I have already indicated its use as 'the white noise' of an acoustical screen; with specific and significant exceptions it was played but not listened to, at all events by my garrison. I myself listened to it as much as I could, save for when it was so inaudible as to be a strain, as in the first period of my imprisonment, or so loud as to be a cause of physical distress, as in the first weeks of my second phase, or so wearisome, by repetition or debasement of quality – as in the last months of my captivity – that I found it better to ignore it.

I have already observed that successive teams of my guards all finished by drawing sustenance from great classical music, or at

least by finding that its constant repetition did not become an
irritant. Unfortunately this sensitivity did not extend to one
particular type of music, of which they never wearied, and on our
repertory of which, with each successive team, as they took over,
they flung themselves with ever refreshed and unflagging zeal.
This was what they termed 'folklórico', but which in practice
was straightforward modern protest-music, mostly though not
exclusively in Spanish. Musically it was for the most part of high
quality, in both execution and composition, and verbally even
more so, if the listener shared, or could render himself temporarily
indifferent to, its total ideological commitment. For the most part
its humour was too bitter and jaundiced for its undeniably high
satirical standard to make much appeal to me, though the musical
quality made it more than acceptable as a background, once it was
reduced to normal volume. A great deal of this protest-music was
received – in my first hideaway – from a local radio station, Radio
Vanguardia, which seemed to specialize in long programmes of
this nature. So much did it appeal to my captors that they taped
whole sequences of it to supplement their already ample stocks of
cassettes and records, many by the same artists. This tape eventually
provided them with an inspiration which, for a while, filled me
with false hopes of communication with the outside world, as
was evidently its intention. It was elaborately doctored to give the
impression of tuning along the dial – particularly of tuning in to a
news-bulletin, and tuning out just as it began. For a long while I
suffered much frustration in consequence and, even when I
decided that it was after all just a joke, could never view it as other
than a very bad one. Where his contacts, real or imagined, with
the outside world are concerned, the captive has no sense of
humour left and is, I think, entitled to this one human frailty.

I can remember the names of many of the young composers of
these protest-songs, but do not propose to quote them; I suspect
that, as the years pass, some of them not specifically and overtly
aligned, or even later publicly identified, with the urban guerrilla,
may not remain wholly enamoured of some of their own extremer
theses and imagery. Some of course were unmistakably participant

terrorists – remote-control activists in what might be termed the intellectual commandos; precisely by its high intellectual quality and content it was clear that much importance was attached to this front of operations. Other composers, authors, performers were avowed participants in the para-military urban guerrilla, one indeed being of its acknowledged hagiography. He it was who had composed, played and sung a touching threnody honouring another and earlier 'martyr', as he saw it, of Latin American revolution, Ernesto 'Che' Guevara, the Cuban revolutionary who later had been killed in a technically most controversial effort to export Cuban-style rural guerrilla to Bolivia. I would not deny the sincerity of the author, in his evident grief for this folk-hero of the Latin American revolutionary young, nor that of his comrades in continuing to grieve over his recent death. What however I had in all honesty to contest was his rewriting of history in terms of his ideology, his poetical and musical presentation of my own country in an odiously familiar and banal stereotype, and his unquestioning condemnation of people of two hundred years ago, for their failure to analyse events, and to conduct themselves, with the hindsight of our own generation, of two hundred years later. Not least significant about a piece of music otherwise sadly revealing of the various talents of its young author, prematurely lost for his country, was its reference to the iniquities of a major United States corporation which – however chequered or controversial its past – had never operated anywhere in or near his own country.

I am always an easy catch for a good tune, and had to steel my heart against the siren-song of one particularly fine but tendentious piece of writing, and rewriting. I remember exactly neither its name nor its author; but its theme was the struggle for the independence of Uruguay nearly two hundred years ago, under their great hero Artigas – 'Capitán José Artigas' the choruses of this work termed him. In particular the composition celebrated the moving exodus of virtually the whole of Uruguay's then minute population, to live in exile and poverty across the great rivers till their liberties were restored. The music and the singing were quite beautiful; but its version of history was wholly suspect, certainly most debatable. By its background of campfire music, with the primitive mandolines made from armadillo-shells and the rhythm provided by a kind of *Schuhplatten* round-clapping, and by the lurking melancholy of Latin American male-voice harmony, the tragedy of the epoch was clearly projected. Whether however the presentation in it of Artigas as essentially a people's pioneer against rival imperialisms and a stagnant colonial oligarchy was honest is another matter.

For the rest, and especially as time went by, I formed the impression that – as contrasted with the content – the form and quality of what was to make up the acoustical screen gained steadily in significance. Perhaps my always pragmatical captors realized increasingly that, as well, it performed a positive psychological function as a soothing background, much as does piped music in a waiting-room or airport of today, and as did palm-court music in the hotels of yesterday. So, from time to time, I would recognize a new acquisition – *The Seasons* of Vivaldi; one of the Brandenburg Concertos; an Argentine folk-singer, so much more authentically bull-voiced than any gaucho as to seem almost synthetic, almost too good to be true, in the best tradition of the Don Juanesque horseman of the Argentine pampas, apologizing for his 'pecadillos', always one fateful breath too late, at the deathbed of his aged mother. Similarly agreeable to the ear though vulnerable to serious analysis of the text, was an ageing American vedette projecting a philosophical mellowness more attributable to his script-writer than consistent with his press-clippings.

As with their reading-matter, I noticed that the music of my captors, the nearer it came to our times, tended to the sad, the negative, the empty, the melancholic, the frustrated. For a while they had a passion for 'soul' music, a form of American Negro song usually again expressive of urban frustration, but requiring considerable skill musically in improvisation, and textually in its verbal equivalent, sometimes, I believe, termed 'signifying'. Another favourite was a recording of an English-language pop-group chanting over and over again the simple words 'Power to the People'. My custodians understood these words, and often joined in. They did not however understand the words of another repetitive song recorded, they explained, by one of a till lately celebrated British pop-group. It had been 'El Elefante' who one day asked me what was the meaning of its insistent theme. In Spanish I replied 'Nothing's Going to Change My World'. Characteristically there followed his short pause for reflection, and a bark of laughter. 'That's what he thinks!' commented The Elephant.

Chapter 18

ALL the occupational therapies which I have so far described have, I notice in retrospect, been of a passive and a receptive nature. Yet since the French prisoners of the Napoleonic War and their wood-and-ivory models – replicas in minutest detail of the ships-of-the-line they had served in – the craftmanship of the captive has been famous, and undoubtedly has been so since human time began, and with it the power of one man over another. I was no exception, in at least intent if not execution; no more so – after I acquired his company – was my neighbour Ricardo Ferrés.

Just as idle hands are reported to attract energetic diabolical attention, so too their occupation by work of great accuracy and detail may be supposed to be of wholesome and salutary effect. Certainly in my own disposition there has always been something of the frustrated artisan; and within a short time of my imprisonment I had invented for myself manual tasks the outcome of which added to my comfort, as their protraction supported my morale. To my amazement I discovered in myself a quite swiftly developing aptitude with the needle, which began with relatively crude tasks but, with time, acquired a considerable refinement, if always in a strictly utilitarian rather than an aesthetic capacity; I can now darn a hole in a sheet to the degree almost of invisible mending, though needle-point embroidery is still beyond me.

It began with the rotting gauze of my first mattress spilling foam-plastic chipping all over my cell-floor. My woman guard was in charge of the housewife-pack, for Women's Lib had not yet penetrated into the world of clandestinity. So a couple of times she briskly sewed yet another gaping seam together. Finally I asked her to pass me the reel of thread and her needle, for a major re-stitching job. There ensued consultation – I assume to satisfy themselves that there was no responsibility should I literally seek to make my quietus with a bare bodkin! Thereafter the materials were left with me, and indeed stayed with me. For as fast as I renewed one seam yet another came apart, till finally I had resewn all four sides and all five panels of my palliasse. I began with a simple, indeed rudimentary, running stitch, which I soon remembered my wife used only for preliminary tacking; the catch proved to be that every time the thread broke by my sleeping head the whole length of the seam would open down to my foot or vice versa, with all the alacrity of a zip-fastener. For a while I dealt with this problem by inserting a locking stitch every few inches. Then I realized that the actual fibre of the gauze-mesh was rotting at the edges; so I devised a system, again retrieved from one of my less sentimental but ultimately now cherished recollections of my wife, of making a large hem, which I then made firm by stitching over it, with a process I later found is well known as 'whipping'. It proved both effective and reliable, but had one drawback. By the time I had made good my whole mattress – and not once but several times over – it had shrunk in width by several inches and in length by about a foot. But at least it held together till I was moved to my new gaol, and, not sleeping on the floor, no longer needed such a mattress.

That I am not exaggerating my prowess when I refer to invisible mending is even now open to ocular proof. My cellular undervest, which served as everything from pillowcase to lampshade and towel, and gradually progressed from white to drab-brown, had one of its meshes caught and torn by a projecting barb of wire. With much patience, a very fine needle, and a thread taken from the hem, I determined – and was finally able – to re-weave it, by copying and reconstituting as exactly as I could the texture of the surrounding 'cells'. This garment, whiter-than-white again, can today be seen in the museum of that excellent firm, Messrs. Marks and Spencers, at their headquarters in London, with a red ribbon leading to, and a magnifying glass flatteringly elucidating, my now regrettably forgotten skill.

At this aptitude I was soon outstripped by my friend Ricardo. A time came when we were emboldened to comment disadvantageously on the design, finish and appearance of the Ku-Klux-Klan hoods affected by our young guards. Defensively they explained that their version could quickly be made by folding diagonally a simple square of cloth and hemming one of the non-hypotenuse sides. Three slits would accommodate eyes and mouth, while the top corner curled over on top of the head like a Phrygian cap, and the bottom corner covered the chin and throat like a bib. That I considered their hood unbecoming my custodians had realized at a very early stage, from the primitive sketches I had made when given my first ball-point pen and paper. It was some time later that they realized that I also saw it as obscurely comic, despite its macabre connotations and indeed intention. This realization represented, in retrospect, a significant watershed in our relationship. In particular both Ricardo and I had realized that they were sensitive about wearing a disguise-cum-uniform which, seen now through our eyes, they recognized as indistinguishable from the trademark of the to them 'Fascist Ku-Klux-Klan'.

So a day came when one of the young men suggested that, if we disliked their hood so much, we might at least be constructive, and try our hand at designing one which would be less offensive to the eye and more functional than the current model. A lady terrorist was co-opted to make styling suggestions. The consensus was that first a square cut was desirable, to remove the *auto-da-fé* inquisitorial look of the Ku-Klux-Klan model; that a close fit to the head and brow was desirable to ensure stability; that looseness over the nose, mouth and chest was essential to combat the heat of the environment; and that reinforcement of all orifices – for eyes and mouth primarily – was needed to avoid the unravelling which reduced the security and durability of existing types.

I think that it was Ricardo who volunteered the inspiration that gussets, or gores, were the solution to the ventilation problem to which our guards were subjected underneath their hoods. Take a narrow rectangle of cotton cloth, fold it in half lengthways, with the closed end sewn half-way down each side, and with a triangle of cloth stitched in at the loose ends, and elegance was reconciled with function and simplicity. The response to Ricardo's proposal bore out that the old adage 'Never be willing, never be efficient' is as true in a para-military and clandestine setting as ever it was in the army. Ricardo promptly found himself supplied with an armful of cheap muslin, needle and thread, plus a great deal of constructive advice from myself through the wire of the neighbouring cage. Within no time at all Ricardo had far outstripped me, in both volume and quality of output, as a seamster, if such there be.

It was at about this time that we were supplied with 'warms' – a sort of baggy trouser or bloomer made of cotton jersey. Known locally as 'bombachos' after the traditional balloon-cut riding-trouser of vaguely Spanish-Arab configuration, this garment was intended to protect us from the short but quite chilly Uruguayan winter. I personally never needed it for this purpose, though its springy bulk provided me for the first time with a comfortable and much appreciated pillow. The jersey fabric also had a remarkable capacity for unravelling itself, especially where doubled over to make a tunnel for the elastic at waist and ankle. Once again my earlier skill at hemming served me in good stead and whiled away much time.

The episode of the 'capucho' or hood had originated in another manual therapy, derived from my earliest attempt to teach myself how to draw. I had often tried to sketch my surroundings, which consisted largely of assorted and superimposed squares of wire netting. My captors were clearly highly nervous of this effort, which they undisguisedly feared had some intelligence or espion-age intention, or at least that of seeking somehow and ultimately to denounce the harshness of my setting; it is noteworthy that neither of my two 'interviews' with outside journalists had even been contemplated in my first and unspeakably squalid gaol, where I was for obvious reasons held totally incommunicado. Only when my captors realized that these sketches were genuine efforts to occupy my mind and hands, and to while away the time, did they relax their vigilance. They did so to the extent that one of my custodians realized that I was struggling with a phenomenon, evidently utterly unknown to me till that moment, named perspective. As a result my beams, girders and floors were all tilting towards a range of improbably varied vanishing-points with a drunken surrealism which my guard – who from his drawing might have been an architectural or engineering student – set out to rectify.

I am grateful to him; for in my second captivity I was able to satisfy myself with a – to me at least – interesting composition of superimposed grilles, bars, and their assorted shadows, to which I sought to lend depth, dimension and life by including in the corner foreground the hooded profile of my guard, crouched reading on his chair in the alcove provided for our invigilation. It is not my fault if his cone-shaped hood, with its slits for mouth and eyes, had a fearsomely satanic quality; I drew him that way because that was how he appeared. When he came to take a look at my efforts he was horrified that this was how he seemed to me. It was at this stage that the move to restyle the triangular hood was initiated.

From the same episode began too another and more fruitful of my personal therapies. Stupidly perhaps, this reaction of my guard made me feel sorry for this particular harmless vanity of his youth and naïveté. So I decided to cheer him up, and his comrades, by launching myself on a whole ambitious series of cartoons or caricatures. I was encouraged in this project by one or two single studies I had made which, despite their crudity, had in their line captured some of the humour I had tried to instil, and which had actually conveyed, if not all at least most of, my intention.

I christened this series 'Normalization'. It conveyed a moral – that the practice of clandestinity was liable to prove hard to shed. But I hoped that I projected it without bitterness or cruelty, and with a certain recognition of its exponents' *esprit de corps*, though with manifest rejection of their motivation. The theme of each drawing was that of my captors, back at normal activity in the real world outside. Life was going on around them as usual. The only anomaly was that they – male and female – were still wearing their cone-shaped terrorist hood. One drawing showed a Beauty Competition for Miss Comrade 19?? – the last two digits of the year, and therefore its proximity or otherwise, were coincidentally obscured by the sombrero of a 'Kildare-was-here' type of figure leering over the back set. 'Les Girls' – Junos, pocket-Venuses, bespectacled studious types, all in their assorted bikinis – still wore their Ku-Klux-Klan hoods, as did too the compère at the microphone, the dog scratching on the beach below, the seagull passing by, and the pilot of the biplane towing a publicity streamer overhead. All save one of my guards found the theme unobjectionable, even amusing. The exception – a lady – considered beauty competitions a mere meat-market, humiliating for her sex and for the Tupamaros. When I explained that I was in entire agreement on principle, she was reconciled to my drawing as an authentic and even amusing representation of an undeniable if meretricious social reality of our times. This was the only occasion during my captivity when I met anything approaching 'Women's Lib.' Relations between the two sexes of my captors fitted as a rule into all the usual contemporary graduations between camaraderie, vestigial Latin American 'machismo' or 'rooster-complex', and even that formidable phenomenon, the aggressive, dominant, utterly Hispanic matriarchalism which can produce a shrew, a Santa Teresa de Avila, or a not infrequent and wholly admirable half-way wifely compromise. Only with a gun in their hand did I ever observe the total elimination of sexual differentiation among these young terrorists.

All the women appreciated a cartoon in the 'Normalization' series entitled 'The Little Surprise', with a slim, and hooded, young man accumulating cigarette-ends in a waiting-room, being warned by a square-built, and hooded, hospital sister what to expect in the maternity ward beyond the partition-wall, where sitting up in bed was a hooded young lady whose mask bore a Gioconda smile, and whose arms a brood of likewise hooded triplets. The men took most to 'The Football Group', a pseudo-photograph where the usual mixture of tall, squat and hirsute players stood, sat and crouched behind the championship cup –

all of course hooded. In addition, when I received a set of felt-tip pens, I did a colour drawing in the same 'Normalization' series, entitled 'Changing of The Guard'. The background was a vaguely institutional residence which my custodians immediately decided should be the Presidential Palace. In the gate was a sentry on guard, in full Brigade of Guards uniform: bearskin: red jacket and all. Similarly clad, but rather overweight, stood to the left a trumpeter, while to the right marched on-scene a relief-guard of four, in close locking-step, graduated from a beanpole specimen in front to a diminutive guardsman in the rear. All participants in the ceremony were however hooded of course! So that it should be clear that I was prepared to mock myself too, the last of the 'Normalization' series showed a vaguely but unmistakably diplomatic limousine parked by the sea-shore, and strolling by it a comely young woman, with a huge smirk on one side of her face and, clutching her hand, a little boy, all knobbly knees and huge eyes, and an expression compounding amazement with gratification. With her free hand his mother was pointing at the car. This time both participants in the scene were at long last unhooded. The caption read in Spanish 'Not YOU, Mama!!' The terrorist was now a wife and mother, and at last had openly admitted her bygone clandestinity.

My impression is that this last drawing was everyone's favourite – so much so that from this time onward it became the practice of all of my guards to ask me to do a drawing for them to take away as a personal souvenir when relieved. I remember that there was one young woman who, at a time when much of my food consisted only – to my great satisfaction – of green vegetables or salads with invariably carrots, gave a clear indication of her pre-revolutionary bourgeois formation by arranging the green-stuff in the centre of my enamel plate with sliced raw carrots assembled tastefully around it. For her I drew a rather Impressionist-style coloured still-life of this subject, entitled in Spanish 'High-Protein'. To others I presented specimens of a set of playing-cards I had devised in minutest detail and colour, with the finery of the face-cards copied as exactly as I could, save that

King, Queen and Knave all wore the terrorist hood, and held in their hand not a sceptre, a sword or a flower but a rocket-launcher, a sub-machinegun, a heavy automatic pistol, a ·45 revolver or whatever weapon seemed suitable, and fitted.

Humanly it gave me immense pleasure that these strange and violent young people, in the midst of their unnatural and bitter life, should take something close to an innocent pleasure in these amateurish attempts of mine, designed largely to distract and cheer my own mind. There was even some slight physical re-assurance in their being requested as take-away souvenirs; I have often wondered too where they found their way and, indeed, may since have reappeared. But I remained under no excessive illusion; more than once, in between drawings, the alarm, the silence, the darkness, and the click and feel of the cocked weapon reminded me that these were but concessionary glimpses of our common humanity, to be superseded at any moment by the larger, overriding, omnipresent and deadly empiricism.

Chapter 19

IN recollection I have decided that it was my efforts at drawing which finally led me to write things down, at first on paper and, in the end, by a form of scanning process, in my mind. Much as I enjoy, and particularly enjoyed then, seeking to execute in terms of plastic art the notions that formulate themselves in my mind, my skill, my training – and I fear my inborn aptitudes – simply are not adequate. In caricature this failing can be glossed over, though I would never say that it does not matter; the greatest cartoonists I know have always been, when they wished, superlative draughtsmen, and vice versa, like Picasso – when he so wishes.

But my cows tend to have five legs. So too, I might comfort myself, do other more distinguished zoological models; I saw *in situ* and scarcely disinterred the Bulls of Nineveh, which as I recall have even six legs. But that was on purpose, and for a good reason in its time; while mine was just an extra leg, and by accident. My pictures have never quite said just what I wished to say, whereas what I found myself writing – like Molière's Monsieur Jourdain and his speaking of prose after many years – was a habit. And – just occasionally – I found that by writing I could convey precisely the exact image and thought that were in my mind. I could accept that what I had written might not please everyone, or even mean anything to anyone but myself but, by my own lights, I had for a moment achieved perhaps far from perfection but at all events an optimum. At least the cow that I had described rather than painted had four legs, and each one on purpose.

So from the beginning of my solitude I had longed to write. For many weeks it was not allowed, and then, for a while, was so far as I could understand logistically impossible for my gaolers to arrange. In my first and unspeakable gaol my eventual materials comprised a cheap ball-point of slight duration and a scratch-pad of the lowest quality – in fairness no worse than what at any rate I saw my captors using, though I suspect they had better material in their part of the wood; and even for a while I heard a type-writer which one of them rashly offered to lend to me, an offer rescinded on, I understood, higher authority.

Obviously the first use I made of my authorized writing-materials – once I had cautiously discovered that the prohibition against anything other than drawing was easing, and that my efforts were not at once snatched away – was to seek to write to my wife. Only too well did I know – as I shall explain – that these letters were a purely academic exercise, and in reality addressed to my captors only, which is why in due course I ceased making an involuntary present to them of my successive drafts. I wearied of their being removed and invigilated, as I did too when I started to write my first children's stories. In the end I gave up writing letters, save for one a good deal later, which I was asked to write but which I found was never sent, as too I soon gave up writing down my stories.

My first story was 'The Oven-Bird'. It was out of sheer affection for this engaging bird that I composed my first story in its honour, and out of affection for the story itself, which had given me much joy and consolation in the devising, that I swore to myself I would give its name to the whole collection if fate were ever to permit me to complete and publish it. The idea of writing about an oven-bird – the familiar 'hornero' of the River Plate builds a clay nest like an old-style outdoor baking-oven – was a direct manifestation of escapism in its most wholesome sense. The oven-bird is very much a bird of space and the open air. I have watched them build on telegraph-posts, in the forks of trees, even confidingly on a fence-post at eye-level, and on the cornice above my own bedroom window. Though noisy, strenuous and possessed of all the solid bourgeois virtues, the oven-bird contrives to be even so something of a comedian among birds; so I decided that to find a theme about him which would provoke me to at least a smile in the writing – and little children too one day perhaps in the reading – should not be too difficult. At the back of my mind also was a charming poem by the Uruguayan poet Leopoldo Lugones which had provided me with a happy memory from my darkness and reclusion; it describes the clay house of the oven-bird with its antechamber and bedroom and its busy, garrulous and bespattered builder, and ends 'I too would wish to be an oven-bird, building my little cottage to a song.'

His song is no sweet one; for the oven-bird is no nightingale. But his story seemed to me a cheerful one, and to my captors too, as they monitored it. They insisted at first that my text should be in Spanish, which was no real hardship to me, especially in the laconic 'dead-pan' style which I was using for a juvenile readership who too, in a peculiar way, seemed to come to keep me company in my mind. After this story my invigilators decided that there was no risk in my writing in English, so my second story – of a local seal-cub that tiresomely preferred steak to fish – was no longer in Spanish. Both drafts did not however catch up with me after my transportation to my second prison. I waited, and asked for them repeatedly, only to meet with evasions; it was never explained to me why my drafts – along with my personal possessions such as wallet, cuff-links, watch, pen, glasses – vanished without trace. My cross however – which I would truly have regretted – I hung onto firmly and successfully, and my missing stories were lodged equally firmly in my mind; like my cross, I was to bring them home with me in their own fashion.

I inwardly hung onto my first two lost stories, and invisibly wrote the rest, by the same straightforward mental discipline. My plank-bed had a plank top, like a bunk, and I would lie apparently sleeping but in fact using the board above before my eyes, like a television-screen, scanning the words across it and almost reading them in my mind. I wrote ten more such stories, going over and over them with the passing months, with all the tenacity of a child insisting on no variation whatsoever in a bed-time story. As a result I was word-perfect in them when I came home; and I have no doubt that if ever the texts of my first two stories were to reappear they would differ very little from the printed version of so long afterwards.

I used the same technique with a few verses which, after many months, I began to write. These I did write down – again for them to be spirited away – but I recited them over and over to myself both for pleasure and discipline and as a hedge against their possible loss. Only in one case did the precaution fail. Five poems ultimately came back to my mind whole and intact, I am sure. But another went astray in my memory – it was a compendium of all the things I had ever been thankful for, of the body, of the mind, of the spirit. I would not quite compare it with Sullivan's 'Lost Chord', for I am sure that it was no 'great Amen'; yet its disappearance frets me, and I still prod at my memory much as his musician too went on hopefully stabbing at the keyboard of his mighty organ.

Of these few poems one came to me in a strange, wellnigh supernatural and certainly improbable way, and was preserved by a technique normally to be relied on to produce certifiable gobbledygook. In my sleep my mind – my sleeping vision indeed – was suddenly filled with the most vivid and perfect of blues. I accept that the experience may have sprung from the most prosaic of causes; indeed, knowing my hosts, their setting and their practices, I am prepared to volunteer that, as so frequently happened, their lamentably precarious electrical circuitry yet again simply short-circuited on them, and that I woke up with the flash imprinted through my eyelids and lingering on my retina. Be the cause what it may, I sat up, banged my head on the planks above me and, for the hundredth time, stubbed my toe agonizingly on the edge of the recess in which my feet spent their night. In consequence I was wide awake when I wrote down a mnemonic for what I thought I had seen in my sleep. Looked at 'in the morning' – or at any rate after some hours more sleep – it still made sense. I expanded my little note, to make my deceptively entiled 'Blues in the Dark', describing some of the lovely and vivid blue things of life and ending:

'Perhaps their blue, stolen from my sad sleeping,
Was just her eyes, from memory's sadder keeping.'

Along with these carefully memorized treasures, I also constantly rehearsed and stored in my mind other intangible but precious disciplines and possessions. They included my contingency-planning for moments of crisis and danger; for the possibility of escape, however remote; and for the chance of saving my life in the event of a shoot-out, or a sweep in which my gaolers might omit to hold a gun behind my ear, or in any such way leave a crevice in the door open for some positive action by myself. In the event, I believe that there was only one such occasion when I was not handcuffed and under a gun; but hope never flags, and I always worked on the supposition that a time might come when it would be worth a try.

For such an eventuality the first priority was to work out some system of staying alive during the peak of action; in particular even the non-participant human frame is exposed to cross-fire and ricochet in small underground boxes made largely of stone and concrete. So in each place I located a cranny where, if not immobilized, I might seek cover of a sort. In my first gaol it was a corner up by my roof, in an angle of the concrete beams which so many times had cracked my head, but which in this way might eventually redeem their obnoxious presence. By using the main beam ostensibly to exercise by practising press-ups, I had worked out a system for swinging myself up, and jamming myself in a corner shaped like a box of reinforced concrete, with only one side exposed to the floor. By suitable contortions all my more vulnerable areas would be massively protected, and only that portion which, despite my loss of weight, remained the fleshiest part of me would be exposed to a chance ricochet or even to deliberate aim.

In my second hideaway I discovered that the concrete floor did not extend into the recess which housed my feet when I lay on my bunk. Instead there was a hole a couple of feet deep under my plank-bed inside the recess, going down into the black earth with a most unpleasant looking small pool at the bottom. It seemed to me that I could just about contort myself into a foetal position which might approximately be accommodated in this well-sheltered corner. Thereafter a further contingency-plan would be needed for egress – more easily contrived I found, for my first and more jury-rigged gaol. The second was so solid as to be almost impossible for me to force my way out with the naked hand; discreetly I had conducted appropriate experiments. And whether for a security-sweep or for a normal emergency there was always the risk of fire to consider. With a most precarious and amateurish electrical installation, and an abundance of dry lumber in their construction, these 'People's Prisons' were a major fire-hazard. At least three or four times during my captivity there were electrical fires of some dimensions – so much so that I suggested the provision of fire-extinguishers, not least in my own cell. My captors thought it a good idea, and claimed to have passed it along the channels. But nothing came of it, and right till the end of my months underground the 'spat' of a short-circuit, followed by not always suppressed profanity, was a routine part of my background.

These overloaded circuits were for the most part on the minor and amenity side of the clandestine electrical network – immersion-heaters for tea and maté, small fans, record-players, home-made and imperfectly insulated lamps and reflectors. In both successive installations I was able however to catch a glimpse of the main power-leads, so heavy-duty as to amount in my second residence to massive copper bus-bars, the sheer technological clandestinity of which must have required a major effort to maintain. The drain on the power-supply by such huge turbines must have been difficult to conceal, even if superimposed on existing heavy industrial plant. If simply bypassing an ordinary domestic meter, I cannot see how it could for long go unperceived by the local power authority, with its effect on the district network and the neighbourhood transformers.

All this heavy-duty ventilation apparatus produced its own characteristic sighing and humming, with especially at 'morning' its own special coughing, popping and backfiring. To identify it became another of my inward obsessions and mental pastimes, though the only occasion when I sought to exchange views with my technically most knowledgeable neighbour Ricardo was met with an instant caveat on security grounds from our guard. In general I soon realized that all serious thinking was best kept within the confines of my own head, a further reason – above and beyond my liking for such privacy as I could retain – for my never having sought to keep a full diary, even surreptitiously. I am glad; for that I should not have cared to leave behind.

Chapter 20

EPISODE, rather than the self-devised sectioning of time which for the last few chapters I have been describing, supplies the captive with the real landmarks along his interminable grey road. And of all extraneous episodes the most lifegiving and anxiously, even tremulously, awaited, is a visit. I have explained that my first visit 'from home' proved instead to be that of a Cuban journalist who arrived complete with prior thesis and *parti pris*. To that extent his visit had been a disappointment, though I cannot but be grateful to anyone who facilitated news of my welfare to my wife, family and government, no matter what their motive.

The second time that I was told that there was to be a visit 'from home' I maintained all my mental reserves, if not indeed suspicions, refused to allow my first excitement to dominate me, and did not expect too much from the intimation that I should be seeing a prominent British journalist.

I was not therefore too disappointed when, some time in the second month after my transfer to my final destination, the small female figure that was led hooded into my cell was speaking fluent River Plate Spanish rather than a halting Anglo-Saxon version; yet another sounding-board for the organization, I thought! My mild disillusion was at once however reduced by one stage, when my captors actually removed my visitor's hood.* It was almost entirely dissipated when I recognized the features revealed as those of an authentic visitor 'from home'. In my confusion I could not recall the name, but the setting yes and with a little help, the occasion.

My visitor was Miss Maruja Echegoyen, whom I had met at a reception at the Uruguayan Embassy on my premonitory visit

* See Appendix 2 for text of interview.

back home less than a year before. I had been told at the time that she was a long-standing member of the small Uruguayan colony in London, and a public-relations consultant who regularly helped the Embassy on occasion. Though surprised therefore to see her in this particular galley, I was unfeignedly glad, and all the more so when she produced some quite excellent apples and a couple of books, one of them a most intelligent historical 'who-dunnit'. I recall that it particularly appealed to me because its hero, though the captive of an injury and not, like myself, of a kidnapping, shared with me the problem of passing time. Weary-ing of mapping the cracks on his ceiling, he exercised his mind by treating an episode of history like some detailed police problem. I was to feel kinship with him, even friendship for him as, flat on my back too, for much of my time, I kept my own mind active while performing that less glamorous part of the ambassadorial function summarized over three hundred years ago by Sir Henry Wotton. He is usually, I am told, misquoted one word short; for, as I hope to be an honest man, I was certainly 'lying hard' abroad for my country.

But at this very moment I was uncomfortably crouched on the low and hard edge of my bunk, waiting eagerly, a little anxiously, to see how this contact with the outside world would evolve, what inkling of the real world without it might give me, and, in any possible way, of my own destiny as well. My visitor seemed brisk and competent, and well disposed. It impressed me favour-ably too that she began with a joke – to the effect that she had had a great deal of difficulty making contact with my captors, and till she saw me was half convinced that she might have been the victim of some monstrous hoax. Knowing well the 'malicia criolla', which might quite conceivably go as far as some vast adolescent spoof or a practical joke of this kind, I agreed that there had been such a risk, but that my visitor could now be sure that my presence at her point of arrival was no joke at all – far from it!

As with my previous visitor, I asked Miss Echegoyen to con-firm her *bona fides*, and she promised me that an unedited version of our interview would be passed to the serious press of the world and, in particular, of my own country. She seemed interested in my childhood and my personal and educational background, of which I gave her an unadorned account, revealing myself to be I fear far too normal and conventional a person to be the centre of so sensational an interview. Like most diplomats, I have been never a man of extreme views, with indeed the familiar and uncomfortable professional deformation of an all too great facility for seeing both sides of an issue.

I was therefore a little taken aback when my interrogator sprang upon me a succession of rather Freudian explanations for my plight on which she asked for my commentary. One was almost of a 'death-wish' category – had I taken no precautions for my safety out of some kind of suppressed desire to be captured? With some sense of outrage, but with no desire to imperil the liberty and safety of my deputy and colleagues by a reaction of excessive frankness, I replied that I had taken all the precautions possible in a then still hypothetical situation. As a diplomat I had no wish to transform my installation into an armed camp. Nor was I sufficiently complicated a person to go in for special motivations. The facts as they were accounted for my story. I had felt no subconscious boredom with my function – to the contrary I only wished that I could reawaken with the clock back where it was on that fateful 8th of January morning.

I may perhaps have been a little too emphatic for politeness, but I was truly amazed when Miss Echegoyen next inferred the existence of reports that I might have been some kind of a special agent planted by the 'Intelligence Service', to be captured and to penetrate the secrets of the Movimiento de Liberación Nacional. So, though these speculations were firmly brushed aside, I made up my mind not to bid my visitor farewell without making sure that no one would be tasteless enough to add to my wife's anxieties by baseless sensationalism of this kind.

I remember too that we discussed my *modus vivendi* with my captors, my unspoken but never abandoned insistence that, on or under Uruguayan soil, I was still accredited to its government, and our reciprocal agreement to differ where our articles of faith were concerned. Hoping that my wife would get to know of it, I described my reading, my personal disciplines, even my diet and my exercises. It was when I proffered my analysis of much modern Latin American writing that I realized a fact which came as no surprise to me. It would have been most unlikely that my captors would have admitted to their inmost stronghold – and much less thereafter restore to normal circulation – a person whom they did not recognize in advance as sympathetic to their aims. Miss Echegoyen volunteered emphatically that she was not herself a participant in the Movement who were my hosts, and it is true that her whole approach was a Roman Catholic 'Third World' view of society familiar and – with certain crucial reservations – even most sympathetic to me. She never therefore 'hounded' me, or sought to corner me, like her Cuban predecessor. Yet even so I had to resist attempts by her to induce me to commentaries on Latin American problems of social and economic justice which would have been an indiscretion for even a captive ambassador. Perhaps because of my obduracy on this point my visitor asked what would my position be if ever liberated – would I be suspected of contamination, of subjection to brainwashing? I think that I laughed, explaining that our British services did not operate on such assumptions, and that I expected to go back to normal work one day. Certainly I remember having to be even more obdurate in my refusal to discuss the problem of justified violence, despite my visitor's insistence that these particular questions were addressed to me as an individual and not as an ambassador. So many times in my life I had explained to pressmen and women that in any expression of my opinion to them I could answer only as a spokesman of my country. I would never have believed that my professional convention was so ingrained in me that I would refuse to shed it even in the wholly unconventional setting of a subterranean terrorist dungeon. The conditioned reflex is usually spoken of somewhat contemptuously. I can only say that I am grateful for the professional reflex which prompted me to answer aright, thereby at least sparing me the nightmare of a professionally uneasy mind, while making the nightmare of the setting that much more bearable.

My visitor – herself evidently a person of broad intellectual interests – was clearly intent on pursuing mine, and their effect on my view of my captors. She had realized that, caring much for history, that of my host country could not have failed to attract me. In particular it happened that I had evolved a distinct fondness for Uruguay's national hero, Artigas, whom I have already mentioned in a musical and 'folkloric' connotation. Artigas is one of history's not uncommon heroes whose grandeur lies as much in their failure as in their measurable achievement. It is perhaps because Artigas failed in so grandiose and protracted a way – with decades of obscurity, exile, even ostracism – that among Latin America's numerous Founding Fathers, Precursors and Liberators he is perhaps the most purely 'simpático'. Because of the lurking mood of grief and betrayal around his triumph and epilogue, Artigas is inevitably an attractive figure to an 'Angry Brigade' mentality and movement; and it was a sorrow to me to hear him adduced by them in a connotation hostile to my country which, to the best of my knowledge and conviction, he had respected and even possibly after a fashion loved, as till recently have most Uruguayans, and as they will, I am confident, continue to do. So on this theme again I believe that I was obdurate with Miss Echegoyen, and used her questions to answer them with a theme ever dearer to me with the passing years. Seen in the light of particular trends and episodes of the time and setting my country has, I believe, for the most part had a better-than-average reaction and record. Detached from the hindsight of others whose own contemporary response was probably far more vulnerable to historical censure than that of the British of the day, my country has amazingly little of which to be ashamed. In Latin America especially I believe that her political, moral, social and economic balance-sheet is a creditable one.

So I made it clear, I think, to my visitor that any incitement to the youth of Latin America to view Britain as an hereditary enemy grieved me. Latin America needs friends, I maintained, and if a trans-Marxist-Leninist approach were simply going to diminish their ranks when the new generation would most need them, then they were the victims of an ill turn. I hope and believe that this largely ethical insistence of mine did not exceed my own self-prescribed limits of internal political 'non-intervention'. Certainly I had to refute, oddly enough, the same allegation made of and to me by my captors, of identification with official Uruguayan strong-arm policies. It remains one of the heaviest crosses borne by the diplomatic representative of an authentic democracy that a courteous aloofness from comment on the internal policies of a receiving government is invariably taken by its opponents as active endorsement.

As this fascinating and strangely nostalgic dialogue continued, I realized that despite myself I was growing very weary indeed, both mentally and physically. To her credit, Miss Echegoyen did not take advantage of what must have been evident, though I did have the greatest difficulty in separating the often almost theo-logical strands of our discussion from what could almost too easily have been the political. Thus from the question of the right to kill of the ordained priest it was only one step to the concept of tyrannicide, or of the justified civil war, or revolution, on which I simply was not prepared to express an opinion which so easily could have gravely embarrassed my government; they were I felt already sufficiently entangled with the problem of their kidnapped ambassador, whom it was, I reckoned, my prime duty to try to restore to them materially and professionally intact, if possible also with honour, and without recrimination.

During the whole of this interview I counted very much on Miss Echegoyen's long acquaintance with Britain to have provided her with a corresponding familiarity with our national turn of humour. On a later occasion – a press conference after my release – I suspect that I must have taxed hers, by classing along with the annual 'invention' of sex by each new input of adolescents my captors' apparently equally original and startling annual discovery that the end justifies the means. But on this present occasion we both conducted without misunderstanding our counterpoint of shared understatement, as when I apologized that I had been unable to obtain the prior clearance of my government before according her an interview of such importance.

It ended on a note to me very moving. My visitor told me that the pupils of a local school with which I had a long-standing relationship and of whom I had become very fond were making clandestine bombs in the afternoon and praying for my safety and release in the evening. My anguish at the first revelation was counterbalanced only by the reassurance of the second with, somewhere in between, a cold anger at whoever could cause these little ones – some of them admittedly a good deal taller already than I – to stumble. I, at the unmistakable receiving end, could vouch for the evil parody which was the reality within this allegedly new morality.

Chapter 21

ALTHOUGH I had met Miss Echegoyen only once before, it had been in my own country, with my wife, and at the home of a colleague whom I had learned to consider a friend. It was therefore with a sensation amounting almost to desolation that I saw her led away, and the door of my cage ostentatiously bolted, and padlocked, behind her. I think that she noticed this so pointed gesture of physical authority. I had in anticipation steeled myself to decline my visitor's kind offer to convey personal messages; I could not see any such gesture bringing warmth or comfort to my wife – rather only, to the contrary, outrage and indignation. But my self-denial, which I hope did not transmit itself as ungraciousness, had taken its effort. In physics one reads of the molecular film and its remarkably tough surface-tension, in science-fiction of equally intangible and impenetrable 'force-fields'. Whatever such barrier it was, that so implacably separated me from all that I loved, was now revealed as only too permeable to those who held the key, or formula. But to me it remained as impenetrable as the heavy-gauge pig-wire which materially surrounded me, however much I chose to make myself indifferent to its existence.

It occurs to me in retrospect that, considering the vast significance of this and my few other extra-infernal visits in so dreary a waste of time, I have perhaps failed to give them their full human and personal importance. This last encounter for example represented a contact not just with mankind but, via the transforming spectroscope of womankind, with humanity, which is something subtly more. On such a journey as this it is inevitably the landmarks that count rather than the landscape, after a while at any rate; not for the first time I have thought of the kinship between the captive and the astronaut, who too must find, despite every effort of will, the boulder in his foreground looming larger than the mountain-range of his lunar backdrapes. So I can only regret it if I have presented too impersonally my sight of the first and last familiar human form – and at that feminine – in all this long and shadowy transit. Some of the blame must in all justice perhaps be attributed to the incessantly blunting and desensitizing influence of the mask, doffed, donned, yet always ultimately sanctioned by its wearer the guerrilla.

It would of course be patent nonsense for me to dogmatize from this particular generalization that, apart from the most natural and conspicuous of exceptions, I have habitually found it almost impossible to tell one woman from another. Yet it is true that, allowing for differences of complexion, eye-colour, articulation, even of structure, the immense majority of women, young and old, can by hair-styling, make-up, colour and style of dress, remarkably blur the native differences between them. So, if I have seemed excessively impersonal in my recollection of so important a visit as this latest, I hope I shall be forgiven if likewise the women of my nightmare days, if my watchwomen, girls and women of the clandestinity, tended then, and tend since even more in memory, to assume something of a depersonalized and composite identity and appearance.

I have since concluded in any case that, with all human beings, it is gesture rather than feature which differentiates and makes memorable. If this generalization is true of us all, and especially of the young, and still more so of the female young, who of us all are perhaps the most conformist in their external nonconformity, how much less must appearance matter and signify when neutralized by the same uniform, of blue jeans, a blouse – as often as not indeed a man's shirt – and a slitted hood? Perhaps coquetry does not go to make revolution; though I cannot believe that it might not go to make revolutions easier to bear and, even in action, to survive them. Try however as I may, I cannot recall one single external instance of reassuring feminine frivolity to give human dimension to this women's underground. Woman's weakness – and even womanly kindness – occasionally yes. But to differentiate between their exponents remained only approximate height and form – surprisingly misleading through bars and grilles – with, still blessedly distinctive, temperament, personality, dogged femininity triumphant over masked anonymity, and now and then heart, even charm.

All in all however the woman of the clandestinity remains only too sadly for me if not a stereotype certainly a composite. One of them once peered through my bars at a sketch that I was trying to draw of my two brothers, who are twins. 'Forgive me', she said, 'but to me they look like a pair of Identikits!' The joke and its double meaning were equally good. So I intended neither bitterness nor affront when I laughed and replied 'I suppose so. But then to me you, who are here and alive in three dimensions, still look to me like an Identitupamara!'

She took my poor jest in good part – better than I can now see it deserved. She was of the good-natured ones – of the majority, I would assess them. One might assume that ideological motivation would prove to be a selective force, and would sift largely the harsh, dedicated and dehumanized of their kind into a terrorist organization; yet the ensuant cross-section, male or female, seems to me to result much as any other human community, at least when not in professional militant action. And the Latin American woman is for the most part good-humoured if sharp-tongued, breezy and comradely with her menfolk, not easily put upon in practice no matter what law and tradition may say and, therefore, not usually given to an inferiority-complex. Just such a woman was my guard – or might have been one day. So I got away, undeservedly I would say, with a poor joke only faintly justifiable by the camouflaged anonymity of the invariable terrorist hood.

Not with all of my women guards would I have escaped with just a laugh for an answer. With one small and ferocious blonde guerrillera I was usually confronted with the conversational option – her option – of either furious silence or aggressive hostility. She had small and almond-slanted pallid-blue eyes, with almost invisible eyebrows and lashes which, in the unexigent setting of a subterranean gaol, she evidently found it unnecessary to darken. She, and one of the doctors who occasionally visited me as a locum tenens, are the only people whom I have ever seen of whom it may be said that their eyes were 'hot', as against the more familiar 'cold'. The doctor's eyes were 'hot' with a kind of mad and bloodshot merriment however; whereas this young woman's simply burned, with fury, blind resentment, hatred.

Why, I never understood. I never had a conversation with her, though on one occasion I was at the receiving end of a nonstop diatribe of remotely economic inspiration. It gave me the impression that her background may have been Russian or Central European since her account of current situations and trends in my country was little different from that which Marx or Dickens or Gustave Doré might have rendered in their time. In particular she was one of those who had accepted blindly the Victorian stereotype. Though to her the words 'neo-colonialist' and 'neo-imperialist' academically existed, the concept for which they stood had not changed in a hundred years. There was no such entity as 'Messrs. So-and-So Limited'; there was only 'The So-and-So Trust'. No evolution in British business thinking and ethic was conceded, but only – at the very most – the metamorphosis of a dripping-fanged wolf, lion or even John Bull into the subtler and superficially less sanguinary updating of a giant octopus. No credit was given for development which could never have taken place without the catalyst of foreign capital, for all its candid dedication to the profit motive. Only blame was laid, and that never apportioned – it was just another monopoly of 'The Trusts'. Within a class definition, this was the most ultra-nationalist of jingoisms, emanating furthermore from a female of the species indeed deadlier than her male comrades, with most of whom one could occasionally discuss these themes without the plastic-curtain equivalent of a slammed door.

Fortunately in my second and final gaol the installation was so much larger, and the transit of guerrilla personnel so much more intense, that these human traits tended to balance each other out: for the occasional archetypal termagant there would always be an equally and oppositely 'ewig-weiblich' ministering angel. This was especially noticeable among the simultaneous three who, from their timing and personalities, I had firmly decided were schoolmistresses, on holiday with the Movement. One of these was a tall, gentle girl with quite lovely eyes which, for once, the abominable terrorist hood could not debase. One of my profoundest sorrows has been the experience that, thanks to the discipline of the hood, I learned to read much from the human eye alone and now, without the hood, to recognize the eye of violence in the streets, shops, parks, even on the television-screens of my own and other ostensibly terrorist-free countries.

It was therefore a profound relief for me to see the 'window of the soul' from time to time opening onto candour rather than the wary opacity which is the eventual mark of the urban guerrilla, male or female. It was also however an immense sorrow to contemplate what could only lie ahead of so transparently kindly and good-hearted a young woman; I had noticed her attitude towards my neighbour when he had been far from well with an abscessed tooth. She was of the same age as my son's wife, and my heart went out to her when, one day, she quietly asked me about them. What a long time, she commented, it would be for her before she could even contemplate the possibility of marriage, the stability of a home, and children whom she could bring up with herself and their father rather than consigning them to grandparents and a whole milieu contemptuous of parents 'on the run'. Even if they were to grow up proud of her, and whoever her eventual husband might be, it would not be good for them to think of their absent parents with nostalgic pride, any more than with shame and a sense of desertion. I had heard so much clinical approval of the 'stable relationship' of the revolutionary text books that my heart softened and my mind marvelled at the deep principle and stoicism of this gentle and womanly child. Whether she had killed, or was to do so, I shall never know; yet some part – I hope all – of her had moved intact through this cruel dialectic and its dreadful environment.

Much the same, in rather less emotive terms, can be said of a contemporary of hers on my guard-roster. This was a brisk and intelligent girl whose mask was less pervious to such beauty, whether of feature or of spirit, as lay behind it. She was comely enough of general configuration – as indeed are most Uruguayan women – nor was there an ounce of ill humour in her either. She lacked the latently maternal essence of her companion, but made up for it in liveliness and intellectual energy. My neighbour Ricardo had by this time become phenomenally good at the 'Numbers' game and, being the only inhabitant of our under-world who could hold a candle to her, she would give him no peace.

Ricardo is blessed with an affectionate disposition and a large family, including an only daughter who is the apple of his eye. I could always tell when his warm heart was stirred by the reflection in this improbable setting of his own intense family life. Many was the time therefore when his face would crease into a resigned but affectionate smile, and the eye nearest to me close in a stealthy wink, when this young woman came bounding into the guard's cubby-hole, pad and pencil at the ready. I knew when, with all her skill, Ricardo was letting her win at the six-digit post-graduate category of 'Numbers' to which they had progressed, just as I knew when he was sacrificing a couple of hours of quiet reading for her youthful intellectual restlessness, or even of much-needed sleep; for even in the stillness of a dungeon one can grow strangely weary.

It was her numeracy, or addiction, which in this lady's case helped me over my chronic difficulty – though I did my politest best to hide it – to distinguish one of these young things from another. It was self-evident enough for even me to identify the day when, without warning so far as I know, she no longer appeared. I was sorry for Ricardo, who had clearly enjoyed his battles of wits; these girls, and their young male companions, had been 'a good batch'. And I suppose that the solitary human soul, alone on its life-raft, anxiously maintaining contact with nearby drifting forms and voices, has the right to regret the departure of the ship that passes in the night – even when that ship is by defini-tion an enemy submarine.

In their alternating appearances over my desolate horizon there continued however to be some vessels more hostile than others, in this female check-list of my self-appointed enemy's flotilla; for my own part I still wished only that they might have left me out of their particular quarrel, although its exclusively localized and regional nature was I must admit growing daily more questionable to me. So I accepted it as a normal catastrophe of nature, or product of the law of averages, when the next tall and lovely young woman's brown eyes overflowed not with womanly compassion but with ill temper, arrogance and simple cruelty.

Once again the mask, or hood, demonstrated its total transparency to authentic expression and character. If technically and aesthetically our new team-mate's eyes were things of beauty, their habitual expression would have petrified a basilisk. It was of little comfort to me that there was nothing personal in this attitude of hers; it was no better with my fellow prisoner nor, so far as I could make out, with her fellow gaolers either. She gave the impression of resenting her role as a destroyer of society almost as much as the destructible society itself, nor did she demonstrate any of the self-conscious idealism and sense of voluntary immolation which seemed to reconcile most of her comrades to the discomforts and dangers of their existence. To me she seemed a profoundly disgruntled, troubled and dangerous human being. I was relieved when, shortly before my liberation, she departed. Later I heard that a fellow prisoner had been located and rescued by the Uruguayan armed forces before his captors could shoot him. Apparently it was the woman guard who had insisted that the standing order to shoot the captive should be obeyed. Her more phlegmatic male companions recognized philosophically that such an action would result in an instant mass holocaust, sought to dissuade her, and finally immobilized and prevented her. The episode had ended with the young lady drumming her heels on the floor in a state of total hysteria.

This was precisely the possibility I most feared in our new woman guard. She lacked the composure for the most part typical of her kind, being instead sullen and unpredictable. One characteristic reaction of hers happened so shortly before my release that, literally, I carried its scar, indeed its smart, back into freedom with me. By the time of my release I had some twenty-six small ulcers, open or scabbed, all over my body, as a result of my run-down condition plus inadequate hygiene. One in particular, in the small of my back, was tiresome, and interfered with my sleep. Finally I asked for a plastic dressing and some ointment. Silently this young woman brought them. After experimenting with the various contortions needed to apply it, I asked for her help. I had already put ointment on the lint. I would pass her the dressing through the netting, and stand with my back to it. Would she then be so kind as to apply it, through the wire?

Without a word she turned her back and walked away. So I shrugged my shoulders and did my best to peel the dressing myself over my sore spot backwards. This little episode was however to have a sequel back in England very shortly; for it happened just before my release. Before taking the aircraft home I went over myself and replaced all the patches that I could see. Those invisible on my back were installed, in an act of true corporal mercy, by my deputy Jim, just before take-off. One, which was just under my lumbar waist-band, escaped his ministration; I suppose anyhow that I had grown used to its presence. Within a day or two however it was under the grave scrutiny of one of England's finest physicians – or perhaps I should say Britain's; for the first alteration in his impeccable professional calm that I noticed was when his soft Hebridean voice came suddenly from behind me with all the fury and sibilance of one of his native wild-cats. 'Who did this?' he demanded. Evidently the gauze pad was on healthy flesh and the sticking-plaster adhering to the open wound. I explained the circumstances; and the episode ended with the classic 'This will hurt a wee bit', followed by Celtic musings on the terrible transformation that can be worked by evil counsel on a decent lassie.

The only comparable problem-child I encountered among the revolutionary womenfolk was no lassie, but quite an old lady – the only elderly person, male or female, I met in all those long months underground. She arrived when we were going through certain medical problems, and gave me the impression of being either a doctor or a high-ranking nurse detailed for observation duty. Her educational level was of the highest, to judge from the standard – and volume – of revolutionary literature which she read nonstop. She took no time off her reading for conversation, and in fact was anything but conversationally inclined. To the contrary, she possessed the attribute, not unusual among elderly ladies, of sparingly interrupting pointedly long and total silences with isolated verbal barbs of a trenchancy and pinpoint accuracy at which I could only marvel. Only from her thin and stippled hands was it possible to deduce her age; her sweatered and trousered figure remained neat and elegant, if a little stooped, and if her movements too were perhaps a little spidery. But her black eyes were still bright, and malicious, and her mental agility formidable. I never had a kind word out of her, yet derived much amusement from studying her technique with its verbal brickbats, and taking evasive action when, with happily decreasing frequency, they came my way. This was a lonely and unhappy woman – a frustrated grandmother if ever I saw one.

Equally small was the last person I shall single out from this gallery of revolutionary womanhood. Neat and wiry in build, she was, I should guess, little more than an adolescent, and bursting with an energy out of all relation to her size. With a certain quality of toughness she had also that of gaiety, and indeed was the only one of my guards, of either sex, whom I ever heard singing. I myself adhere very much to the old adage that sorrow finds a swift release in song, though most of my vocal efforts tended to be across, or even at times adjusted to, the incessant accompaniment of our musical background of 'white sound'. This young woman tended conversely to choose the odd interstices in this virtually nonstop programme – during the ritual of 'ventilación' for example, or when the air-turbines were being rested. I have often wondered whether she might not have followed this pattern with some long-term arrière-pensée; for in remarkable circumstances, which it is not now the moment to describe, she was later to amaze me by conjuring up a totally unexpected and strangely relevant piece of Percy Grainger's music.

So in general I found the women of the clandestinity in temperament much like their sisters of the world outside – perhaps a little more matter-of-fact, with normal vanities and frivolities inevitably set aside, despite their for the most part touchingly lovely figures which were almost all from which to judge their true appearance. Ill humours were, if anything, below the accepted female norm in this environment of stress.

Yet I must confess that, far too often for my liking, I had to listen to weeping in the night. As much as to any man a woman's tears are a distress to me, even if they are shed by my gaoler, or for that matter by my enemy, which by no means all of them set themselves out to be. The saddest instance I recall was a change of shift which, in accordance with the usual familiarization procedure, had the new team brought by to 'see the animals', as I irreverently termed the routine to myself and, in due course, to my neighbour. Usually this advance scrutiny was followed by the first guard-duty, on which the young women were a little self-conscious and stiff, in compensation being sometimes a little aggressive, more often however a trifle loquacious, seeking to make my acquaintance with the same invariable questions which I tried always to answer with rigorous courtesy, unflagging interest and unfailing fresh surprise.

On this occasion the child – she was no more – who came back to perch on the guard's stool in the cubby-hole between our two cells was a figure of sheer and pitiable panic. To my lay eye she was in shock – pale, sweating, trembling, looking away from me as if I terrified her, and shying like a frightened horse if I addressed even a word to her. After my last meal of the 'day', I had arranged as usual my shirt over the lamp, and drawn the flimsy plastic curtain which one of my male guards had unsolicitedly installed at the head of my bed; by gradual 'infiltration' these and other techniques had progressively attenuated some of the rigours of my subterranean 'night'. This night however was to be otherwise disturbed.

I can only assume that the source of the unremitting and quite harrowing sobbing that went on during all our sleeping-period was this newly arrived girl, and that she had been catapulted into the clandestinity either by events beyond her stamina and control or by an over-precipitate decision which she was now lamenting. Comfort, admonition, the offer of tranquillizers – nothing could quiet her. She snuffled, sobbed, and crescendoed into screams for her mother. It was only silenced when, with breakfast, there were sounds of unaccustomed activity. Clearly there had been an emergency appeal for her to be taken away. She did not reappear. I asked what happened and, as occasionally and unpredictably occurred, received an answer – 'The comrade was temperamentally unsuited to the clandestinity,' I was told. What I never knew, and have often since wondered, is whether there was anywhere for her to return to, and a mother who would accept her. Much earlier I had overheard the masculine equivalent of a not dissimilar situation when one of – at that moment – my all-male gaolers had just received and was reading aloud a letter from his fiancée. The phrase 'grunt with shock' had always seemed a figure of speech to me, till this young man came to the sudden and brutal phrase 'I am abandoning you to your useless struggle.' Yet again I wondered if I must be the impotent witness of a young and valuable life destroyed.

Whether it was irrevocably so on another single and most distressing occasion I can only guess. Perhaps it was simply a question of the absence for some operational reason of the usual chaperonage of a high-density barracks community. There was fighting, hard breathing, whimpering, creaking of woodwork and, finally, silence followed by noisy and prolonged weeping. True, it has been said that every happy marriage is preceded by a fortuitous episode of near-rape. On this occasion I fear that there was the reality with little prospect of the ceremony, and that some poor girl had simply been talked, and man-handled, into 'serving the cause', against not only her better judgement but her inclination and principle too. Only on this one occasion was there any indication of my captors' departing from their usual faintly prudish attitude to sexual activity. It had been explained to me that indiscipline and excess were frowned on by the Movement in every connotation. Drugs, alcoholism and promiscuity alike were regarded as dangerous and anti-revolutionary personality-flaws. I could only sadly assume that on this occasion the Old Adam had prevailed, in the absence of conventional group-therapy, with its age-old consequence of human diminishment, bewilderment, and remorse. If at times I had found my hosts, like so many revolutionaries, a little too oppressively bourgeois in their overt behaviour-patterns, I could have wished that their human fallibility might this once have chosen less classic an instance to deploy itself.

Chapter 22

IN this long aside on woman in the clandestinity, one personal response impresses me in retrospect, to which it has seemed necessary to call attention. It is the patience with which a captive accepts a certain repetitiveness in the establishment of a relationship with his custodians. To his constantly rotating guard he is a novelty with each change; they much less so to him. This contrast applies with both male and female guards, and indeed, to most manifestations of communication and conversation with them. The same themes tended to repeat themselves with successive teams of young Tupamaros as the months dragged by.

For that reason it has seemed to me most realistic not to treat conversation as episode but as a phenomenon, and to bunch together its recurrent themes as they asserted themselves down the months rather than possibly repeat them, in chronological order. One merit of such an approach is the perhaps rather sad one that it may rectify any misleading emphasis on the moments of humour of my situation into which I may have strayed. It is hardly unnatural that the desolate and anxious course of life in a dungeon should stimulate over-compensation in pursuit of survival. So humour and its present after-image have tended to select themselves involuntarily as looming largest among those milestones and monuments which broke up my drab landscape, and over so long a time.

To the contrary, consideration of the thinking and conversation of my captors extensively, as a pattern and a process, brings out rather its sternness and solemnity. Over the months the moments of spontaneous light-heartedness, so memorable in recollection, add up in reality to pathetically few. It is a sad truth; for such instances of spontaneity could reveal among my captors, briefly and individually, some quite charming human beings poised, it seemed to me, on the brink of transformation into robots. It is perhaps no exaggeration to say that when they acted in terms of ideology, dialectic, empiricism, they were already robots. When spontaneity took over, they were human beings once again. For this reason I have consistently abstained from any charge of serious deliberate cruelty against individual Tupamaros. Any cruelty I may have encountered was not so much deliberate and personal as inherent in the implementation of their teaching. For the same reason I have feared the consequences when, in due course, many of these young people realize, in some eventual setting of normality and spontaneity, just what they did, however clinically and impersonally, to innocent victims.

In successive conversations on the theme of my own captivity I consciously refrained from playing up my own status as innocent victim. Some of my gaolers – and even more so my visitors – tried occasionally, as will be seen, to impose on me the opposite view, that I was some sort of a quasi-war-criminal. In that case I strongly rejected any such suggestion. To resist even the slightest inculcation of an inward sense of guilt seemed to me essential in the preserving of my integrity as an individual, the conditioning process in the counter-sense being a notorious and classic totalitarian confidence-trick. But the rejection of guilt and the protestation of innocence seemed to me utterly different postures: active and passive, positive and negative.

Frequently my guards took the line that I must be philosophical. The phrase they most used with and of me after a while was 'chivo emisario' – scapegoat. I had had bad luck, they said, being available as the sacrificial victim in a situation in which the end totally justified my present discomforts, however unmerited, as the necessary means of achieving it. For my part I left them in no doubt that I preferred to dispense with a form of sympathy which, however well meant, I found disparaging. I remember that I took down my one-volume 'Complete Shakespeare' and found in Act Four of *Macbeth* the scene in which Lady Macduff confronts death saying:

'I have done no harm. But I remember now
I am in this earthly world; where to do harm
Is often laudable; to do good, sometime
Accounted dangerous folly: why then, alas,
Do I put up that womanly defence
To say I have done no harm?'

My custodian took no offence, and agreed through the wire that
Lady Macduff had shown the stoicism of a proper man. I also
recalled – though this time strictly to myself – that King David,
that expert in the finer nuances of solitary confinement, had
consistently reserved for the privacy of the night the making of
his bed to swim, and the watering of his couch with his tears.
Vis-à-vis his public, he meticulously preserved the more spartan
image, that

'I will not be afraid of ten thousands of people
That have set themselves against me round about.'

Though therefore opposed to the pleading or protestation of
self-evident innocence, I felt no inhibitions about down-to-earth
complaining, though never about trivia. My most serious single
complaint came towards the end of my first dungeon spell, and
was not in fact intended as a direct protest. I had been discussing
with a visitor – a brisk young man with a light and pleasant voice
which I am sure I heard in charge of the pistol held on me during
my subsequent 'transportation' – our material and environmental
problems. I accepted – and he rather perfunctorily deplored –
that our damp, filth and stench were shared. We all used the
same grey, sopping towel, the same crusted plastic toilet-bucket,
the same scum-stained and tide-marked wash-bowl. To such
details of material discomfort I could adjust without outrage.
Similarly I was not disturbed by solitude – in the circumstances
even to the contrary. But what I could not tolerate, as a profound
human injustice, was to be treated as a 'bulto', a package, as –
even though a captive – a 'do-this-do-that' cypher, deprived of

answers to questions which had no ulterior significance. After a
few more instances of this kind of psychological and intellectual
quarantine, I suggested that they of all people should be the first
to concede that humanity, in or out of gaol, should know no
second-class citizens.

My visitor seemed interested, and we discussed the point
further, but academically and not as a special complaint submitted
for attention. A few days later however the 'curtain-raising'
ritual which I have already related was instituted. It was one
manifestation, I was told, of a new relationship prescribed on the
highest authority. Seized of my criticism, it was explained to me,
they had taken it very ill that there should be the slightest im-
putation of deficiency on the score of their compassion. I was
therefore to be awarded henceforth my fixed minimum ration of
human company, and in other ways to be treated as an animate
and thinking creature.

Not all my efforts at self-assertion, and at the conserving of my
identity, met with quite such study and even, after its fashion,
understanding. From the very beginning I had internally devised
my own 'Four-Point Plan' to keep my inmost core intact. Once
I had formulated it I invariably recited it to myself on awakening
and sleeping, and during my 'day' too, if ever I felt that my
morale was flagging. It went more or less as follows:

(1) I am in a totally passive situation – a prisoner, guarded and
immobilized. It is up to me to turn this into an active situation,
by seeking survival through the preservation of my health and,
when it comes to the point, my life.

(2) I am in a totally negative position – no freedom, no family,
no friends, no news, no time, no light, no faces, no green growth,
no world. It is my obligation to turn all these negatives into a
positive by identifying in them a purpose, pursuing it, and attain-
ing it.

(3) There is no reason to hate these people (my 'hosts'). Nor
however may I be sentimental about them. I must therefore make
no concession to them, and give them no satisfaction.

(4) These people, however objective I force myself to be, have

done my family, my government and my country an immense injury. I have no right to add to it by anything I may do, and conversely the absolute obligation to seek by any means I can, to transform that injury into a good, for my family, my government and my country.

This Four-Point Plan served me very well as a private admonition when things looked bad.

There came however a time, very much later, when I decided that it needed some appropriate externalization. I had been in my second dungeon for several months when we had what I suppose I can this time rate as a 'bad batch' among our successive guards. To be addressed by my surname alone, though discourteous in a Spanish-language setting, and from young people, had never particularly disconcerted me. To be addressed by the most of my captors as 'amigo', no matter if only superficially – or ephemerally – intended, had obscurely comforted me. Actually thereafter to be addressed by Miss Echegoyen as 'Ambassador' had seemed some incredible echo of an unreal past. But to be brutally addressed as 'Number Ten' by one of this latest batch, from the numbered tin plate on the beam across my door, was more than I was ready to stomach. I said nothing in reply. But, on a large sheet of my best white paper, I set to work to engross, in my finest chancery script, or the nearest to it that I could achieve, a diploma-like document comprising my personal 'Code'. It consisted of a form of decalogue, beginning to the effect that:

(1) This cellar is not a People's Prison.
(2) To the contrary, this is the British Embassy so long as I remain in it.
(3) I am not the People's prisoner.
(4) To the contrary, I am unjustly held captive, being guilty of no offence against any man.
(5) I represent in this place a great and honourable nation, which is a force wholly for good in the world.

I should perhaps have felt a great deal happier, or less furious, had I known at the time that a day was approaching when I should be able to incorporate that same fifth sentence in my acknowledgement of a 'welcome home' telegram from my Prime Minister. Meanwhile however my self-hortatory tablet-of-the-law continued along progressively self-righteous and claɪɪon lines ending, as I recall, with a tenth self-admonition to preserve my fitness of mind and body, so as to resist any unjust assault on the dignity of my person or my country.

With the assistance of my kit of assorted felt-tip pens I got to work around the edges of this I suppose uncommonly pompous document, so as to incorporate into it an adornment of oak-leaves in green and gold, or at any rate bright yellow, interspersed with an improbable collection of red and white roses in honour of both aspects of my North-country origin. The botany of all this adornment was as dubious as its stylization; but I thought that it looked eye-catching, and passably medieval too after I had illuminated the capital letters with pale blue. There was a further trace of private satisfaction secreted in the first pencil-sketch. Tucked away among the scroll-work and arabesques was a third calendar, as a fall-back to the other two that were disguised on other papers I kept, in case I should ever be separated from these vital links which I was trying to maintain with the element of time. For such purposes I usually amused myself by thinking the words in English, mentally translating them into German, and writing the German out in Arabic characters camouflaged as a doodle or an adornment.

The *magnum opus* complete, I wedged it into the woodwork, so that it hung after a fashion on the wall of my cell, took two steps to my door, doubled back the soft tin of the home-made 'No 10' so that it turned in against the beam and out of my sight, stepped back to my bunk, sat down, folded my arms and, with profound satisfaction, awaited events.

These were not long deferred. The guard in the sentry-box outside was reading, and took some time to notice, and to call his tiresome comrade. An outraged shriek announced to 'Convict Number Ten' that he had most heinously damaged the People's Property, and that I had insulted them into the bargain by my offensive graffiti. By this time a number of curious heads were craning round the corner, some of them – to their credit – with unconcealed amusement. I stated that it was about time to re-establish a few neglected conventions. First, I was a person, and not a number. I would not answer to a number. Further, I had not previously wished to make an issue of the number-plate inside my cell-door. But in no self-respecting gaol anywhere in the world was the number other than on the outside of the door, for organizational convenience. A number on the inside of the cell-door was therefore only there to impress – or depress – the occupant. It was a form of psychological assault which I was not prepared to tolerate, and if they turned the plate down again, I would simply double it up once more. These comments represented my formal request for my objections to be submitted to the Political Command.

As so often, taking a stand with my young gaolers seemed to diminish irritability and stimulate their on the whole considerable intellectual curiosity. They became very interested in my 'Ten Commandments' and, though disagreeing with most of them, conceded that they represented a useful framework of belief for my particular purposes. They made not the slightest effort to remove them, so I left them up till they began to grow a little shop-soiled. I then put the sheet in a large 'folio' I had contrived, from which quite frequently I was asked to produce it to satisfy the curiosity of some newcomer or visitor.

It is possible that this episode had to do with a curious by-product of my imprisonment which was brought back to me afterwards. I gather that much of what I did and devised was collated, and described to other prisoners of whose presence I was unaware. One of my gaolers hinted as much to me in fact. Yet it is an expertise which I should gladly have done without, and which I most earnestly pray I shall never have to deploy again.

This particular conversation about my personal 'drills' was fairly explicit. In various ways our captors had indirectly indicated both to my neighbour Ricardo and myself their approval of our relative imperviousness to the adversity which had become our lot. Only rarely however did they betray any outright recognition of this fact. From his comment therefore that I had devised a useful pattern of self-sustainment I was able to talk to this one of my gaolers about their own loyalties and articles of faith.

He placed great emphasis on loyalty to the group. Not for the first time I noticed a 'Boy Scout' quality of earnestness which, quite naturally, was the more pronounced the younger its proponents were. Much of it corresponded to authentic idealism. Some part of it, again all the more concealed by youth, was no more than sheer old-fashioned tribalism, or Latin – especially Latin American – dedication to the cause and, particularly, to the cacique. Quite unconsciously these various elements were, it seemed to me, serving the most old-fashioned of power-struggles. Its older participants had clearly realized already that, having committed themselves, they now had an enemy whom they must destroy lest he destroy them. In this process their solidarity was vital to them; and on more than one occasion Tupamaro leaders – like many other captured urban guerrillas – have declared that in captivity, as in expectation of execution, they have been sustained only by the certainty that their comrades were continuing the struggle.

More than one of my guards had admitted to me that solidarity and indestructibility were their greatest strength, since they could place no foreseeable time-limit on their struggle. As long as a People's Army was needed, they would have to continue intact and unimpaired. They were 'The People Under Arms', and would continue as such even, for example, if an authentic People's Democracy were to achieve a political victory. They, The People, would remain vigilant and under arms, to move in if ever necessary as the expression of the People's conscience and will.

I commented that I knew of no government, least of all one based on the Marxist-Leninist pragmatism that the withering away of the state will take some reaching, which would leave military power in the hands of a force uncontrolled by the political executive, or vice versa. My guards could not see this. The Tupamaro's dedication to his weaponry is total. Politically he is 'imprinted' by his weaponry. I cannot believe that this is an accident. His – or her – intellectual leaders cannot be unaware that the human instrument which they have forged for the conquest of power has this strange, mirror-image Boy Scout allegiance and, almost, gun-fetishism which could one day be its own death-sentence. I cannot see any totalitarian regime tolerating for a moment the perpetuation of a parallel and armed supervisory body. In such circumstances I can see only two prospects for the rank-and-file Tupamaro. The first would be to achieve personal 'room at the top' via a classic power-struggle, which the senior Tupamaros seemed to me already to contemplate. The second would be their early liquidation, as having served their purpose, which to their idealism, however lethal in its immediate term, was evidently inconceivable. I listened to them with sadness, asking myself at what point does martyrdom degenerate into vulgar cannon-fodder. And who, in this dreadful place, was the true prisoner?

'Be absolute for death' was a forgotten but multifariously apposite phrase from *Measure for Measure* which I had rediscovered in going through my underground Shakespeare. At first I had perhaps egocentrically considered only its application to myself. I was trying very hard to stay healthy, and alive, yet was reconciled that I was permanently but the crook of a finger away from death, though not necessarily agreeing with Shakespeare that 'either death or life shall thereby be the sweeter.' It soon occurred to me however that what he had in mind had an even crueller, indeed far more sinister, application to my young custodians. I myself had only to stand up to immanent death, and face it. They had to pursue and challenge death, in act or anticipation, every moment of their day. And no matter how they rationalized their situation as a 'just struggle', as an undeclared war, as a para-military action, as in short the urban guerrilla, their position can never in truth be compared with that of the soldier – conscript or volunteer – in formal and codified warfare. To him death is part of the deal, to back into reluctantly, not to rush into lemming-like.

I did not wish to impose on my captors, even internally, mentally and to myself, the affront of now attributing to them some form of a 'death-wish'. Yet it did seem to me that there was a morbid and anti-human quality in their fatalistic pursuit of a long-term aim which many of the best – like El Flaco of my earliest days with them – did not really expect to live to see ful-filled. Much of their thinking, and reading, had a noticeably heavy existentialist content. I wondered whether the new mor-bidity displayed by most of these young people did not derive from Sartre, Camus, and their numerous River Plate emulators who seemed to provide much of my hosts' reading.

In so many of these young people I believed that I could dis-tinguish a familiar mixture, admirable as long as contained within wholesome limits, of fatalism with human dignity. Only when the fatalism began to assume the manifestation of an addiction did its inherent morbidity take command of the personality. The addiction, it seemed to me, was to violence, to destruction, to negation and thence, by ineluctable extension, to death. Here, I felt, was where their movement – and they – parted company with the martyrs and heroes of recorded history. True, they were prepared to fight, and to die, as so many of them explained to me, so that others should benefit. Yet they fell short of true altruism, or so it seemed to my perhaps over-subjective vision, because too many harmless eggs were broken to make their particular omelette. Many heroes of the past have bloodstains on their hands. But when Robin Hood, El Cid, even the great modern commanders, shed innocent blood, they did so with a sense of sin and regret, by mischance, even marginally, but never coldly and in accordance with the precepts of Machiavelli. So my hosts were, I concluded, reviving the most ancient of blasphemies under the cloak of an already discredited philosophical fad.

Small wonder that more than one of them winced when I took my courage in my hands and asked them how they could live with the ghost of Dan Mitrione. The most honest of them admitted that his death had been decided by vote, a near vote, its results accepted in advance by dissidents who nevertheless, I could clearly see, could hardly bear to recollect the occasion.

Chapter 23

IT will be evident that the course of my various discussions and conversations with my captors ran very erratically. Sometimes it was a question of temperament – with some there was a clear disinclination to talk. Other times there seemed to have been a directive in the sense of taciturnity, revoked after a while.

Just occasionally however there were outbursts of completely spontaneous enthusiasm for which, equally unpredictably, I was occasionally given an explanation. Twice for example I was roused by wild cheering and huzza-ing behind the plastic and hessian frontiers of my territory. On one occasion I was refused, though good-humouredly, any explanation whatsoever. On the other occasion I was told that my guards had been notified by a visitor from without that some fellow Tupamaro had invented some sort of cheap, easily made and efficient rocket-launcher, or bazooka. They claimed that this discovery represented a major break-through in the development of their fire-power and the deployment of their resources, and merited a celebration. So much so that they were going to open a bottle of red wine, of which they offered me a glass.

I received this explanation with interest but some scepticism. The celebration was far too emotional for an essentially technical achievement; and I have always suspected that it was to do with some spectacular moment of triumph, such as a major gaol-break, by members of the organization previously arrested. There were one or two such escapes, both from the main penitentiary and from the women's prison, a particularly significant one shortly preceding, and possibly in part explaining, my own eventual liberation. The jubilation which I overheard would certainly be accounted for much more logically by this kind of emotional solidarity, akin to that which I have already mentioned as alleged by the urban guerrilla in captivity towards his fellows still active in the field.

In any event I declined, as always in my captivity, the offer of a glass of wine. My explanation – that I was not drinking – was simple, and perfectly true. My reasons were however rather more complex than the basic and genuine one that I did not think liquor – even wine, which I most of all enjoy – a good physical and mental accompaniment for so unnatural a condition as close confinement. Still more so I regard wine, and the gesture of sharing it, as an accompaniment of friendship. Though it was being offered to me in a friendly spirit, its dispensers had, however impersonally and vicariously, appointed themselves my enemies, and were at that moment causing profound grief and anxiety to my wife and son. Little indeed did I know how much; for at that very moment they had had no news of me for many months, and were being led to believe me dead.

This internal and almost intuitive resistance to spontaneous congeniality went a stage deeper. Once again, it had to do with the gesture of bending down and reaching through a sort of chicken-hatch, unavoidable in order to eat and live, but repugnant as a social gesture. I did not like taking this decision, for it is of my temperament to respond warmly and positively to kindness. But it seemed to me that the *modus vivendi* which I had established with my captors should not extend so far as an almost ritual manifestation of reconciliation. I must not allow the fact that I could feel pity, and occasionally something very close to affection for certain of my gaolers, to override their profound offence against me and mine.

Of the extent of this offence I had been ineffaceably reminded by another and early conversation, with El Elefante. He had been surprised to find out how much I knew of, and appreciated, Latin American music. It emerged that he was a practitioner himself; from our discussions of guitar techniques and other musical arcana I should judge a good one. He also disclosed that in his Tupamaro capacity one of his functions had been to penetrate the foreign embassies in Montevideo by means of musical groups –

'conjuntos', as they are called. It is true that it is standard practice to enliven a social occasion, and give it a typical, traditional and folkloric flavour by hiring a group, usually of university students who can use the ready cash, to provide a musical background or to sing popular and amusing songs. Do-it-yourself music has always been and remains a normal accomplishment in Latin America, and the Uruguayans have a particular native wit which lends itself well to this form of entertainment. I knew of many ambassadors and other foreign diplomats, who would invite such groups to add gaiety to an evening reception, in return for pocket-money and free drinks. So I was not taken aback when El Elefante added slyly that he had seen me at more than one such occasion. 'Not in my Embassy!' I countered. 'No,' he replied, 'but you would be surprised to know where.' In fact I did, but preferred not to say. This was only one of the countless techniques of detailed reconnaissance employed by the urban guerrilla. Techniques have much evolved since the early days, when two briefcased young officials in a skyscraper-lift could actually be two guerrillas executing the stop-watch-checked rehearsal of an assault on the radio-transmitter occupying the penthouse. Teams of recruits can be given month-long assignments compiling and collating the minutest detail on a potential target or victim. I have no doubt that many an embassy's musical soirée has culminated in some precise and ample architectural and logistical homework by the erstwhile performers.

Given thus that most of my custodians were students, it was natural that from time to time our discussions should be on the economic theme. All the more was this so since, for a time, much of the reading-matter they brought me consisted of economic analysis, and the textbooks written and recommended by their dons. Equally naturally, its contents, and its authors, were totally committed, and presented an exclusively Marxist-Leninist interpretation of the economic world. With my philosophy I was prepared to look at this interpretation and then back at my own, for purposes of comparison. My guards, to the contrary, gave the impression of being exclusively hypnotized by their pre-set ideological approach. In consequence it proved impossible to enliven an argument by trying to inject any hypothesis that did not fit *prima facie* into a dialectical framework.

I well remember, for example, a discussion in which I asked my opponent to consider the possibility that Uruguayan beef was an indefinitely renewable raw material, not an exhaustible mineral the reserves of which could be depleted. To the contrary, my hypothesis was that good husbandry, and the best foreign co-operation, could actually increase that resource faster than it could be depleted. But such a possibility cut straight across doctrines of neo-imperialism and the class-struggle; so a promisingly juicy argument ran out into the sand. Similarly every effort I made to ascertain what my captors contemplated in terms of economic unity for a Latin America unified in – and putatively by – a classless revolutionary society came to grief on their contempt for the current 'capitalist-inspired' Latin American Free Trade Area. I had expected them to envisage a situation in which generation-old fears of economic absorption by Brazil, or political absorption by Argentina, would evaporate in the warmth of ideological identity. But, once again, these young people showed no real, profound, managerial interest in any phase beyond the apocalypse. I still remain mystified whether this apparent blindness, or at least myopia, corresponded to pure pragmatism and dedication to the first-things-first of revolution, or merely to boredom with anything which was not the actual making of violent revolution.

I had no such intellectual disappointments with the most engaging character and personality with whom my captivity confronted me – with the possible and rather different and subtler exception of El Flaco far away at the beginning of my long subterranean interlude. This cheerful and candid young man of my final captivity was one of the few of my gaolers who was not only not from a university – or even an educated – milieu, but was definably and avowedly of working-class recruitment – and of all things a carpenter at that. Petiso – Shorty – was his underground nickname, for self-explanatory reasons. His two main characteristics were an all-embracing obligingness, and an irrepressible talent as a born clown.

Petiso was also a born volunteer, with no resentment of or reserve in this innate reflex. He could no more stop himself from offering his help for any purpose or service to his fellow guards, or to me, than he could stop himself from talking, which he did incessantly, never boringly, and always hilariously. It was he who, within twenty-four hours of coming on guard-duty, had ascertained that boiling water in a hot container, and with a fresh tea-bag, made a totally different product from mere hot water, a cold pot and a second-hand tea-bag. Within no time he was pirouetting on one leg round the corner of my cell, like some improbably hooded Chaplin, with a tray and cup precariously balanced on the palm of one hand, and swooping to a halt with a stentorian call of – in Spanish – 'Here comes the té à la Englis-man!'

Petiso was a great one for making things, requested or not, and for preference out of wood. If one of his colleagues, especially one of the young women, was lifting or carrying anything, instantly it was 'Let me do that!' Not all of them reacted too well to what some of them seemed to consider his importunacy. As a result he seemed to me a rather lonely person, and to suffer – if the notion does not seem ludicrous in such circumstances – from a trace of class-conscious disdain in the attitude of his companions towards him. He was certainly of an affectionate disposition, and to me what his fellows seemed to treat as naïveté could much better be named candour. In our short time together he wanted to talk more about himself than any other of my custodians; and what he had to say did him no discredit.

His function before taking to the clandestinity seemed to have been among his fellow workers; he gave the impression that some such personal liaison was needed at shop-floor level, virtually to interpret for his more intellectual companions. It interested me to see that though, intellectually speaking, there were no class barriers at the level of militant action, they did seem to exist at the level of communication. All Tupamaros were ready to shoot, and be shot at; but not all could talk, or be talked to. Something had happened at this stage to Petiso. He had been found out, and had had to take the clandestine road suddenly and unexpectedly. He had only just been married, was missing his young wife badly, and could not foresee just how or when their reunion would ever be possible. To have a home and a family was his wildest and most cherished dream, and I can only suppose that his clowning and almost hyperthyroid activity were a courageous sublimation of a deep and incessant distress.

Petiso was there one morning, and was not there an hour or so later. To leave quite unheralded in this way was most unusual. As a rule it was possible to sense even a day or two in advance that an upheaval was preparing itself in the guard-roster. But Petiso simply vanished, and after barely a week on duty at that. He had not shown himself 'temperamentally unsuited' in the sense of the young girl of a few weeks earlier – to the contrary, he had settled into the underground environment with the extrovert adaptability of the classic British Tommy. There had to be another reason.

I have always assumed that the hierarchy must have decided that he was falling excessively under my influence, certainly taking a liking for me which they considered a security-risk. Petiso was of a transparently good-hearted and affectionate disposition, and with all the intuition of an uncomplicated mind. He had instantly sensed that I bore him no ill will and, to the contrary, felt great sympathy for him and his absent wife. It was only one further step for him to realize that my detestation of rationalized violence extended to its intellectual authors but by no means necessarily to all its practitioners. Some of these I saw, and see, as just as much a victim, and a captive, as I was. For Petiso to observe and ruminate over my concept of himself and his movement could to his superiors have only been potentially most subversive. So I believe that he was put out of harm's way before he could be contaminated by my bourgeois idealism. Petiso is another of those who I pray has not had to grow older with blood on his hands and murder on his soul, and whose children I would hope to meet one day. I wish him the success he deserves in a decent society, and for him to know, should he ever read these words, that with a proper cup of tea he made a friend.

A near-friendship of another sort was cemented after a most unpromising initiation. The start of my imprisonment was marked by a surfeit of medical attention, much of it of an intrusive kind symbolized by the ever-present hypodermic needle. Then, for long months, there were only routine medical checks with intervals of even several weeks. Only towards – had I but known it – the end of my captivity did the pace of these medical visits pick up once more.

After the first few days were over, only once did the personality of my regular visiting 'practioner' vary; I indirectly gathered that for a while he had been unable to make his way to our subterranean gaol for reasons of his personal safety. For that once only therefore he was replaced by the strange, older, 'hot-eyed' doctor I have described who, incidentally, caused me much discomfort by wrongly diagnosing – and manhandling – what I knew was my old enemy from rowing days, a chest hernia. My regular clandestine doctor would never have made this error. But though I never doubted that I was in the hands of an outstandingly gifted professional man, at the beginning the less I saw of him the more I liked it.

The fault was only part mine. He was a tiny, delicate birdlike man with, as so often happens, an authoritarian temperament out of all proportion to his size. He was also well-read, highly didactic, and brought with him to our first encounter the most impressive set of built-in prejudices adding up in effect to an acute personal hatred for me. After briskly performing his professional function he chose to waste no time setting about me, as so often happened, on straightforward economic grounds. The degree of prejudice in his analysis did his intellect no credit, and amounted to pure and irrational venom, which I was not ready to tolerate. I concede that my response was not such as to endear me to him, or to rectify the wrong foot on which our relationship had clearly started. Nor could I have the slightest suspicion that this angry hornet of a man possessed any such thing as a sense of humour.

So I announced flatly that, just as he was a professional, so was I. I had not, I stated, permitted myself the liberty of lecturing him on medical themes, nor on his interpretation of the Hippocratic oath; I could only assume that he regarded Hippocrates as a vestigial bourgeois sentimentalism, like so much of tested human history to be jettisoned, after several thousand honoured years, in favour of a great step backward into man's prehistory, disguised as a giant advance into the future. Conversely, I myself did not accept to be lectured on economics by my doctor. I had sat at the feet of Maynard Keynes – though I forbore to mention how remotely. I was a trade-promoter by profession, and, doctor or diplomat, I believed that in our circumstances the amateur should respect the professional on his own terrain.

I assumed that the instant and silent departure of my underground medical adviser meant that I should thereafter find myself inscribed on some other practitioner's panel. If it was not so, after my outburst, part of the reason may have been simple luck. As I recall, the next time he came I was amusing myself by a sort of time-motion study. The Tupamaro emblem is – as with many such movements – a five-pointed star. It had offended my sense both of aesthetics and of efficiency to see how many different variants of their 'brand' my hosts could produce. All day long they were drawing them – on the walls and on the woodwork; squat stars, lean and lop-sided stars, top-heavy stars. I had just worked out that it was possible to produce a Tupamaro star of consistent uniformity, and in one stroke, without removing one's pencil from the paper – or more probably nowadays one's tar-brush from the plinth of the Pietà or Apollo Belvedere.

I had just therapeutically completed my tenth or so successive and faultless version, which starts with three criss-cross lines depicting what looks like a simple folding camp-stool, and continues how I had better not say. I was interrupted by a laugh. 'So seditious a pastime for an ambassador!' said my doctor's voice. We had no further trouble. His sense of humour had a grim side, and he enjoyed one manifestation of my own. I had not been well before one of his last visits so, as he left, I told him that I had a leading question for him. Could he assure me that I was not in fact dead and, though not in Hell – I wished no offence to my hosts – certainly in Purgatory? I could be quite positive, he replied, that I was myself, alive, and in remarkably good shape. I thanked him for this most welcome reassurance, but went on to add that it would mean even more if he could confirm it by the issue to me of a certificate to that effect. 'Certainly, Ambassador,' my doctor replied. 'But of course you will understand, and excuse me, if I don't sign it!'

The last time I ever saw him was at my request. I had been sleeping badly, largely because my heart-beat, which I could hear amplified by my hard wooden bed, had become disturbingly irregular. For the first time too since my childhood I had fallen out of bed – or off my bunk, to be more exact. To add to the discomfort of finding myself on the concrete, with my nose caught in some heavy-gauge wire mesh which for a moment I could not quite recollect, I had also in the process once more stubbed my toe, in its permanent state of partial recuperation, on the sharp corner of the recess into which every night I slid my feet like a letter into a pillar-box. I had also had a nightmare – one of my two regulars. In one, my Mephistophelian Tupamaro guard in his cubby-hole would at long last remove his Ku-Klux-Klan hood, revealing a crude face of baked clay, which he would in its turn peel off in sections, leaving just a skull beneath. My other nightmare was that I saw walking across the free corner of my cell half a cat – the back half. So one way or another I was momentarily very sorry for myself.

The guard who saw me fall turned out to be the tall, elegant and embittered young woman who was so unco-operative with my self-administered first aid for my ulcers. I told her that I seemed to have a most peculiar pulse and would be grateful for a cross-check. She paid no attention. In that case, I demanded, I must see one of her male companions, who appeared without further bidding. I explained that I felt perfectly well, but that there seemed to be this strange heart-rhythm – I remember I produced a laugh from him by describing it as six-eight Viennese

Waltz time. If he could confirm that I was not imagining it, then they had better pass the word along the line to their doctor, in case it had any particular significance for him.

The young man took my pulse, and agreed that it was acting strangely. The young woman came back – in tears of all things – and gruffly explained that she thought I had just been trying to make things difficult for her. Next day my doctor appeared.

Fortunately my symptoms had not in the meantime vanished, which tends to be their way when one is nervous of having made a fool of oneself. The doctor observed them, laughed, and slapped my shoulder. There was nothing organically wrong whatsoever with my heart, he explained. These were simple and wholly benign extrasystoles. I was living in most peculiar and unnatural circumstances. My conscious mind had accepted and even dominated them. Not so however my subconscious mind, which strongly resented them. And it was my subconscious mind, or at any rate its physiological instrument, the sympathetic or vegetal nervous system, which controlled such automatic full-time operations as the beating of my heart and the breathing of my lungs. I need not fear that, for example, by over-exercise I had re-activated some former lesion of which, in fact, there was not the slightest trace on the elaborate electro-cardiographs which he had just taken, on some highly compact and ultra-modern equipment which he had brought with him.

I remember feeling greatly reassured, and commenting that praise be, I was not therefore coming apart. 'No,' he answered; and to my amazement added 'You have only one malady, and her name is Evelyn.' He also mentioned my son. This for once purely human analysis of a situation prompted me to lower my guard far more than I had ever allowed myself. I agreed that my concern for my family, and the ignorance in which I knew they lived about my welfare, could not wholly be thrust to the back of my mind. 'There was a fine European musician', I added, 'who fled from the Nazis to America. Perhaps not everyone takes his later music so seriously as his earlier. He wrote some very successful jazz, possibly with his tongue in his cheek. Some people call it "corn". But out of corn is made wholesome bread. And I see no falsification or fraud when Kurt Weill reminds us that it's a long, long way from May to December, and the days grow short when you reach September.' The doctor jumped as if stung. 'Good Lord,' he said in perfect English – 'you're quoting "September Song"! You'll have October, November, December, January and more with your Evelyn with a heart like yours!' Then he stopped, confused, and continued in Spanish, and on more mundane clinical matters.

PART FIVE

THE RETURN

Chapter 24

GEORGE ORWELL describes how a certain quite jejune mass-produced song lodged itself with disproportionate significance in the sentiment of the hero of his *1984*. The memory of the *Threepenny Opera*'s author merits I am sure a loftier analogy and tribute than such a comparison; yet the tune and the incident remained strangely with me, and always will. Only with the skill of hindsight do they assume any sharper significance, and this not necessarily authentic. For this conversation with the Tupamaro doctor took place – so far as I can recall – many weeks before other incidents began to accumulate, and to breathe onto a flicker of hope so tiny and vulnerable that I cupped the hands of my imagination around it every time, lest even the faintest undue stirring should cruelly extinguish it.

I began, after a long and sterile interval, to receive a surprising number of apparently fortuitous and disconnected visits. One was the same breezy young man who, I am sure, had often called in after effectively sitting on me in the truck which had brought me to where I now was. He wanted me to write a long letter to my wife. I was reluctant to do so on demand, having spent weeks fruitlessly writing and rewriting earlier versions, which had always been turned down flat. Finally I agreed, with profound and, in the event, justified scepticism. My wife, of course, never received it. I was inwardly convinced that my captors only wanted me to write in depth and at length for the insight such a letter would give them into my own thinking and state of mind. But the French do say that once we are at the ball we might as well dance; so I decided to enjoy composing my letter. It was of course in the mandatory Spanish, and I recall very little of its detail. At two points my captors were angrily convinced that I was using a code intended to denigrate and vilify them. One was a reference to, I believe, the Third Psalm, intended to convey, with more brevity and elegance than I myself command, my general state of placidity. Unfortunately it goes on to refer to one's enemies being smitten on the cheek-bone, not to mention their teeth being broken. A similar misunderstanding marked my attempt to synthesize my feelings about my separation from my wife with one condensed reference to Shakespeare's Sonnet Number Twenty-seven. Regrettably my invigilator was unfamiliar with the Roman numerals used in this particular edition, and found his way unerringly to Sonnet Number Twenty-eight, which laments being debarred the benefit of rest, and refers to enemies that 'do in consent shake hands to torture me'.

Texts in hand, I was able to vindicate my good faith by pinpointing the authentic texts, which I believe impressed my censor, even though he or some other authority never finally let them pass. Perhaps they were guided by some subtler inquisitorial sense, that armed them against the one point at which I had cheated, despite my own assurances to my wife that in any eventual message from me out of bondage she need not look for double meanings. I can only suppose that it was a combination of misguided humour and the captive's human longing to 'beat the system' which induced me to announce that recent material improvements had produced 'un todo mucho mejor'. This last phrase is, I flatter myself, distinctly stylish in Spanish, if perhaps a little mannered. Translated directly into English it reads loud and clear that I have been translated into Bruce Bairnsfather's famous First World War 'Better 'Ole'. Innocent enough, since Tupamaro hideouts were even then notoriously subterranean. So there was no breach of confidence. But my wife never had the chance to smile which I guessed she so sorely needed.

It was long afterwards that the same young man, with his usual blend of brisk efficiency and poised self-confidence, let himself into my cell and simply said 'Write something. Anything. On any piece of paper.' I produced my ball-point pen and he said with a slight and unusual irritability 'No, no. In ink, in ink.' Patiently I explained that I did not run to such luxuries, and that he had better try one of his comrades. When he came back with a handsome Parker I had decided that, if I was to give a hand-writing-sample with fresh ink, it must be for some purpose of verification. The chances were thus that it would come the way of my government and, consequently, of my wife. Instead there-fore of a hurried 'Quick brown fox' or some similar hasty stereotype, I scribbled down in Spanish and English: 'Darling – These young people are getting so amiable that the only thing left for them is to turn me loose!' The young emissary glanced at it, laughed and disappeared. That same piece of paper is in front of me now, and was with my wife within a matter of days, the chemistry of the ink and its contents proving conclusively that only days before I was alive and in good heart.

Shortly after the same young man came to see me again – for what I no longer recall, perhaps because the substance of the visit was driven out by its exceptionally unpleasant atmosphere. For some reason he reverted to the long-forgotten theme of my 'criminality'. He used of me the phrase – insofar as I can remember exactly any so convoluted an epithet – that I was 'institutionally guilty of the symbolic crime of international neo-colonialism'. By this time my sense of humour was threadbare, but sufficient remained for me to accuse him by return of bad Marxist-Leninism. No less an authority than Vladimir Ilyitch Lenin him-self had, I reminded him, affirmed that sophistry was the most heinous of the Marxist deadly sins. What he had said of me was the purest sophistry, and would not even stand up to verbal let alone semantic analysis. Not for the first time, he laughed, and went away mentioning casually that I was shortly to expect an important visit from a photographer which, in my mind, I identified with the writing-specimen.

But he had in practice accused me of being a political prisoner, which I had understood was not in fact the Tupamaro view of me. Since then I have indeed heard that to other prisoners they con-sistently stated that it was in this way that I differed from them – that unlike them, I was not a political prisoner. So this shift of the kaleidoscope left me a little despondent and perturbed.

Almost immediately however something happened to dispel, or at least override, my brief despondency. In a moment of relative silence I heard the voice of, I take it, my small and wiry young woman guard singing, but without words, the familiar title-phrase from Percy Grainger's 'English Country Garden'. Over and over again, behind the hessian walls, I heard this phrase being tra-la-la-ed till, finally, I could not restrain myself and joined loudly and inharmoniously in at the phrase 'In an English country ga-arden'. There was a peal of laughter, and silence.

But the next morning, at the famous routine of 'la ventilación', as I lay curled up in my blanket against the chill of whatever un-seen apparatus it was, suddenly, right against my ear and through the thickly padded ear-flaps of my ungainly helmet, a girl's voice sang in an almost inaudible whisper, and to the exact phrase of Grainger's music, 'A-and don't forget your ga-arden. A-and don't forget your ga-arden.' For three days this happened, and I waited in a wild hope. But then it stopped. The author of this most welcome of all music I ever heard did not reappear. So I decided that it had been a pleasant hope while it lasted, and put it out of my mind. Wrongly, I believe; for if hope deferred sickens the heart, the absence of all hope can wholly wither it. But happily I did not have to wait all that longer; so here is another one who shall never want for my prayers.

The photographer, who was not long delayed, was of a very different species. Technically competent only in the sense of speed and briskness, I wondered what he was really after. His briskness amounted to brusqueness; I did not like the heavy-handedness with which he pushed his Movement's emblem into position over me; and I revolted when he started to give me orders. For the first time in many a long month I proclaimed that I took orders from no one save the Government of Her Majesty, whose Ambassador I was. 'You know what I think of you and your Government,' he replied. 'Perhaps too I should tell you what I think of that Majesty of yours – Mierda!' he added, which needs no translating even in these days when the unprintable is no more.

This was perhaps the acutest of my moments of truth. A truce of sorts had been breached, and neither time nor finesse must be wasted. 'So you say,' I answered. 'But I would have you know that without that lady, my Chief of State, whom you have just affronted, and without her father, you would have grown up a Nazi. And from the impression you have encouraged of yourself, I don't doubt that you would have made an excellent one.'

There followed the inevitable and brisk altercation. It was promptly joined by a couple of my guard-roster. I thought that it was time to reassert our basic if limited non-aggression treaty. We had contrived all these long months, I claimed, to co-exist in intolerable circumstances, and with the shadow of violent death never far from any of us, entirely because we had mutually refrained from contesting each other's articles of faith. They had never heard me speak disparagingly of their Movement, nor of its emblem, nor of any of the symbols of their patriotism which I knew had a mystic significance for them. In the British concept of patriotism the Crown held just such a mystic symbolism as, in any Latin American nation, do the Flag, the Anthem and the National Liberator run together. Through an accident of history we British have no National Liberator, or even a Day of Independence, incomprehensible as this may seem to any Latin American. And fond as we are of our Union Jack and the National Anthem, they are essentially familiar and friendly appendages of our ordinary life. Above all however to an ambassador, who is its personal extension overseas, the Crown embodies our history, our liberties and their continuity, in the one single principle surpassing even the considerable personal and family significance of the monarch.

My guards did not let their visiting colleague down. They did not allow themselves, any more than I had, to grow heated in discussing so sensitive a theme. I myself had been at pains to retain that expression of countenance known, I believe, as *gravitas* which is expected to be of second nature to the British diplomatist discussing matters of substance at moments of tension. Nor did my young men do so badly. They explained to the visitor that my account of our relationship was accurate, that he was not to

have known it, and that I would undoubtedly be satisfied with a
return to a more impersonal level of conversation. The photographer explained rather ingenuously, if still a little gruffly, that
having had nothing to do with kings and queens, it had not
occurred to him that they were under that designation a functioning Head of State, and the constitutional embodiment of the
national dignity and honour.

In the circumstances this response seemed to me an amends of a
sort, after which its originator got on with his business. He set
up tripods and floodlights, hung reflectors, stood on stools, and
clicked away taking picture after picture with his expensive
Japanese machine. My recollection is that my neighbour Ricardo
witnessed none of these proceedings, having been hooded and
screened off before the proceedings began.

I had soon put this experience out of my mind; and already too
the irrational hope stemming from the single phrase of conventional English song had withered. One day however I had just
finished my 'breakfast' when Ricardo was told abruptly to face
the wall and don his helmet. Two strange young men were
admitted into my cell. They were not wearing the trunks or jeans
of my guards but normal street clothing, and of quite heavy
winter weight. They stared at me silently. Finally one addressed
me. A curious mannerism he had stays in my mind. Unlike
Demosthenes with his pebbles, he sucked barley-sugar non-stop,
I imagine to obscure his voice, which I may have recognized.

'Jackson', he said, and paused. 'Jackson, what would you say
if we told you that we were here to liberate you?' An immense
convulsion went through my whole body, though I hope and
believe that I did not even blink. During all those interminable
months I had been meticulous to the point of prudery in my use
of the Spanish language. But when finally I made myself speak,
slowly and calmly, it was to say 'I should first ask if you were
fooling me' – and I admit that for the first and last time I used a far
earthier word. Soberly the other visitor replied 'Oh no we aren't.'
'In how many days?' I asked. 'Now, in five minutes.' 'Can you
give me your hand on it?' I demanded. Silently both held out

their hand. The hand of one was dry, the other's dripping wet. 'We will get you your suit,' one of them said. It was brought in, dry again but indelibly stained with mildew.

Instantly I implemented a drill I had rehearsed in my mind more times than I can say. I put my surviving shirt over my coarse pink prison shirt; after serving as a night-time screen for my eyes, during the 'day' it was carefully folded on the top 'bunk' alongside my books. I unhooked my Cross from its nail and, in anticipation of the usual travelling contortions, placed it not around my neck but in my shirt pocket, firmly wedged there with my only other surviving possession, my filthy and wilted but still treasured blue silk spotted bandana. I took my shoes from under the head of my mattress. I was ready for the unbelievable journey back – I prayed – to reality and to life.

Chapter 25

WHEN one of my visitors took out from his pocket a bandage of sorts for my eyes I was not disconcerted. I had not seen my way into my dungeon, and still less, was I to see my way out. But first I asked for a moment's grace, and quickly scribbled a brief and, I hope, cheering and affectionate note to my companion Ricardo. So many times we had each or both been futilely required so to lie, face to the wall, wondering what was going on about us. I wedged my little note in the wire, hoped that he would be allowed to find it there, hoped that soon he too would be following my path, hoped that I was in truth going where I hoped – never has so much hope concentrated and superimposed itself within me.

Hope faltered however when, having been steered blindfold through my cell-door and round the corner into my custodians' unseen sanctum, I was told to lie down on what seemed to be a sort of wooden hurdle. My wrists and ankles were tied down to its corners. I tried to encourage myself by the conspicuous absence of the usual concomitant to proceedings of this kind – the detestable Tupamaro butterfly handcuff. So I was inclined to give my captors the benefit of the doubt when they assured me that these elaborate arrangements were devised simply to carry me where I could not walk myself. And indeed for some short minutes I was so carried, head up, head down, feet first, sideways, up ramps and down steps, with heaves and with grunts. I could not help recalling my arrival, and my easy if somewhat over-elaborate walk down to my underground hideout. Either my egress was being still more over-elaborated, or I was leaving by some quite different route.

Soon the cords holding me were loosened; they had held firm

during and despite certain anxious moments, when I foresaw myself slipping head-first backwards down sundry steps and ladders. But now I was made to sit on the edge of what felt like the back platform of a small station-wagon, and told to swing my legs up and huddle down in the space behind the back seat. The bandage was removed, and replaced by a pair of wire spectacles, their lenses taped over with surgical plaster. I was told that I should need to wear these for just a few more minutes of indispensable security; and the motor started.

With every passing moment and fresh little episode the likelihood seemed to me to diminish that this was just one more cruel hoax – or perhaps indeed the cruellest deception of all. The mood around me too was new and strange. With each recent movement there had been a change of quality in the atmosphere surrounding me. The hand pressing my shoulder, keeping me below the level of the car seat, had a different feel to it. The voices that were whispering earnestly to me – one by now a woman's – had another urgent, almost friendly quality. This, they said, was the most dangerous moment of all – not least for me. All must go smoothly or be lost. When the car stopped two of them, they explained, would walk me – arm in arm and chatting like three good friends – to what would be the side door of a church. I must get inside without a second's delay. Then I could wait; they undertook to advise my Embassy.

The moment soon came when I swung my stiff limbs over the tail-board of the station-wagon. In my featherweight suit, donned for high summer and now worn again, after the turn of a year, in the chill of a late spring evening, I shivered, perhaps from emotion too. And, for all my still undigested 'breakfast', evening it was, indeed night, when at last my glasses were peeled off my face.

It was a rather run-down street, nor did the church looming ahead of us seem particularly prosperous; few in Montevideo do. I was walking unhurriedly between a young man and a woman; faces they had at last, but with dark glasses, and I barely recall them. But they smiled sincerely, laughed, bobbed their heads like a horse on a rope, and gestured with their free arm as we strolled along, arm in arm in the old-fashioned way of good friends. Nor did all this warmth seem entirely feigned.

We passed the wide, locked, double door, and stopped in front of the usual small side door leading to the sacristy and the priests' quarters. I found myself instantly alone, and pressed the small tarnished bell-button. As the door opened I stepped straight inside from the now deserted street, and closed it behind me, to the obvious bewilderment of an amiable bearded young man in lay clothes who enquired as to my business.

When I asked to be allowed to speak to the Father, the young sacristan explained that he was briefly absent at a parish meeting, but would not be delayed. I might as well sit down and wait for him. After a moment I asked if I might sit in the body of the church, and the young layman kindly switched on for me one single frugal light which suited me, and all my thoughts, very well. Ten or fifteen minutes must have passed until I was joined in my quiet front pew by a young priest who clearly was mystified by his strange visitor till, in the briefest words, I made myself known to him. He was a sturdy, jolly young man, who took first things first. 'You are shivering,' he said. 'Take my sweater.' I was glad of it, and its warmth let me think more clearly. 'Out here,' I suggested, 'I could soon represent a problem to you.' Instantly he invited me to follow him, and literally I took sanctuary, in the sanctuary no less.

I shall never forget Father José María Senatore, although I have not yet written to him, nor sent any other message than my thanks and a white sweater to accompany his own clerically sedate turtle-neck when I returned it from England. He will understand. I find it difficult to write to Uruguay as yet; perhaps the writing of this book will make it easier. Father José María is a good and kind man. He understood the sadness which my long separation from the sacraments had caused me, received my confession at once and gave me communion. As a practical man, he also very promptly gave me a cup of strong, hot, sweet black coffee, and the luxury of relaxed discussion on ordinary things. These included my renewed contact with that wonderful

element, so taken for granted, of ordinary time. The good young
Father showed me his calendar; it was eight o'clock on the
evening of the ninth of September 1971, instead of mid-morning
of the eighth, as my own assorted calendars had prognosticated.
An error of thirty-six hours in three-quarters of a year's dead-
reckoning was, I concluded, nothing to be ashamed of.

We were just engaged in the infinitely pleasant exchange of
such amiably unhurried considerations when the sacristy door
flew open like that of any Western saloon in a Late Late Movie.
Poised in the door, sub-machinegun at the ready, was the archetypal young lieutenant, clipped moustache, black mirror-lensed
sun-glasses, just as I have so often and so wearily seen him from
the Levant to Central America and the River Plate. He was a
child, no more and no less, no more and no less so than my gaoler
El Loco of a few months before, down to and including the
ultimate pose and angle, and to the last millimetre of trigger-
happiness. But there was nothing there for the boy to confront
save a priest, a middle-aged communicant and an altar. Slowly
the familiar round eye of his machine-pistol lowered its deadly
gaze. A final crisis of some sort was clearly past and safely negoti-
ated.

Gruffly but correctly, as one scarcely used to a voice only
lately broken, my young rescuer invited me to proceed for my
'interrogation'. Patiently I explained that ambassadors are not
susceptible to interrogation by the authorities of the country to
which they are accredited. When he seemed unhappy I assured
him that his superior officer would confirm my assertion, which
he instantly did by a most providential appearance as if from
nowhere. At last I began to feel that the world of normality was
re-forming itself around me, an impression totally reinforced
when, suddenly, my own staff were there and with me.

Chapter 26

S TILL more did the wheel seem to have turned back when, after a final grip of the hand from Father José María, I found my vast official Daimler awaiting me at the church door. As ever, it was as black and shiny and capacious as tradition is alleged to have decreed for our supposedly top-hatted diplomatists. Its scars seemed to have been repaired; the bloodstains had been cleaned away. Yet as I sat down I could not but notice, as though they were unreal, two bullet-holes, one in the hide of the seat and the other in the felt roof-lining. Each was carefully preserved under a small panel of thick transparent plastic.

Nor was our departure any less noisy than on the last occasion. But this time, instead of receding gunfire and the recurrent thumping of a torn front mudguard, it was the self-important bellow of sirens and the acceleration of a heavy motor-cycle escort.

From this moment onwards my usually quite trustworthy memory succumbs to defeat. For about forty-eight hours faces and events fall into a type of shifting montage, much like the preliminary to a television news-bulletin, with snippets and samples of the whole shifting, splitting, superimposing, zoom-lensing. First there was the battleship-grey stillness of a room in the British Hospital, with preliminary good tidings of my physical condition which I was able to retail, incredibly, to my wife, whose voice from the heart of Sussex was on the telephone almost instantly. Formal visitors – even the most eminent – were adamantly kept at bay. Our gallant attempt to enter the Embassy surreptitiously via the gardeners' gate failed through the perversity of one inanimate object, a key surely deliberately gone errant. The front gates, and flash-bulbs. My staff in tears. Bread-and-cheese, and a glass or two of plain red wine. An inspection of the new decorations, and of the longed-for portrait of Lord Canning which, before my disappearance, I had claimed as essential for an Embassy situated in Calle Jorge Canning. Not till the early morning was I put to bed, like their own baby, by the youngest member of my staff and his wife, neither yet of my own son's age.

It was through no trick of diet or circadian rhythm that I was fresh, ready and up for the dawn, but simply at the clamorous behest of a subconscious which, however free it knew I was again, reminded me that I had still not seen again the light of day. I heard the unmelodious voice of my oven-bird, of whom I was soon to write out the story imagined in my captivity. I explored the garden – with aid and escort, less for safety than for my still unsteady legs. Maro, our immense grey tom, emerged from the shrubbery – and no doubt from one of his habitual disreputable vigils – to greet me as though I had scratched his ear adieu only the night before. There were still violets under the lemon-trees.

Back indoors I found my flight home already cleared, and my suitcase packed, in prescience of this occasion, by my wife on her own departure nearly a year before. A carousel of faces rotated before me – most of them much-loved friends, though not all succeeded in penetrating the cordon drawn round my home. The essential official callers – no more – passed by too. I sent a message to Ricardo's wife. Again I was climbing into my Daimler, to the tears of our household, and after I know not what farewell words a full heart led me to speak briefly at last to the fistfuls of microphones thrust over my doorstep.

The 'dear colleagues' lined up at the airport behind the gentle old Franciscan, our Dean; I bade them farewell with sadness, though perhaps looking one or two of them a little hard in the eye.

At last the quiet of the resting aircraft, though not for long when the press moved in on my compartment. The Spanish pilot promptly moved me out into the crew's own little cubby-hole, where I sat hard-seat till I fell comfortably asleep, awakening next morning on the floor, curled up around the table-legs in the greatest of ease. Buenos Aires, Sao Paulo, Rio de Janeiro, Las Palmas – all had flickered before me like a high-speed film, distinguished only, and barely, by the kindness, and greetings, of my local Service colleagues. Finally a long descent, at the pilot's side, across the very Cadiz from which Columbus had set out nearly five hundred years before to prompt all my adventures as well as his.

As we slid down the last descent into Madrid this kind and courteous Spanish gentleman quietly passed me a scrap of paper brought to him by one of his crew. It simply said that a British Government jet was awaiting me at Madrid with my wife, my son, and his wife. Within minutes, as I sat quietly waiting for the turbines to whistle to a standstill, the aircraft door burst open, and I heard my son's voice, suspiciously brisk. We were right next to the neat Hawker-Siddeley twin-jet; and there was my wife.

There were colleagues too, with whom the Bay of Biscay passed in a flash. As we made our landfall the radio-operator passed to us greeting after greeting from the British aerodromes below – a latterday electronic version of 'past Ram Head by Plymouth, Start, Portland and Wight', to remind me of how many a forebear returning up-Channel must have felt his heart lift too. And a mid-air message inviting my agreement to set foot again on my native soil with a changed address and style – as near I suppose as a non-soldier can aspire to the honour of a battle-field award. I was reduced to total and untypical silence.

Below, Sussex was in gala array – a July noon postponed for us to mid-September. Gatwick Airport, with a quiet Palace spokesman, and my own 'master', my Secretary of State. A dais, where his self-eclipsing laconicism vanquished whatever cat had got my tongue. It was as well, for to my dazzled eyes the skyline seemed as battlemented with cameras and microphones as my London square is with Victorian chimney-pots at twilight. The words that followed may have been lame, but were from my heart – even though at the end they must have filtered through the intermediary of my head, being finally demanded in a multi-plicity of languages.

And, at last, the hedgerows of England; my wife's hand in both of mine; and the reality of that English country garden, last conjured up so improbably underground by an invisible singer at the world's other end.

Within bewilderingly few hours of leaving my 'People's Prison' in Uruguay I was leaning my elbows on a split-oak fence-rail along the Ladies' Mile, above the little village of Withyham in the secret triangle of Sussex. I looked out, across England's southland, at its most beautiful in the precious last days of high summer. Down below in the valley, that little stream was the headwaters of the Medway, itself a part of my country's history.

Nearby, in the refuge of her brother's family home, framed by the enduring black-and-white of five-hundred-year-old oak, under a roof like a Persian carpet, was my wife, and my son with his wife too.

I had forgotten that this was September. Quite suddenly my thoughts went back from this lovely and affectionate country-side, to a hooded little birdlike man, in a dimly lit cellar far away, quoting back at me the over-proof nostalgia of an émigré European's 'September Song'.

In two hundred and forty-four days and nights I had not shed a tear. Nor would I now. But for five full minutes I could not speak a word.

APPENDIX 1

Leopoldo Madruga Interview
(interviewer's questions in italic)

When they took the bag off my head I could not only breathe better, I could see a man stretched out face downwards. He was quite strong, rather tall, wearing light blue shorts and a pink shirt. He was lying on the lower of two bunk beds which filled almost the entire cell.

By the door there was a number – 10 – and a portrait of José Gervasio Artigas [the founder of modern Uruguay]. A single yellow bulb hung from the ceiling. One wall of the cell was made up of wire-netting, covered by a patterned curtain. Behind the wire netting was another prisoner, Dr. Guido Berro Oribe, Uruguay's Prosecutor-General.

The three Tupamaros, also hooded, who led me to the cell, arranged themselves as best they could: one sat at the foot of the bed with a tape recorder, another sat on the floor with a notepad. The third sat behind me. 'You can turn around. Ambassador,' said one of them.

Behind the reddish beard and moustache I could hardly recognize the face of Geoffrey Jackson, whose photograph has been widely published. He sat on the bed opposite me.

He seemed unworried, perhaps a little surprised, and his eyes betrayed a certain anxiety to communicate with the first journalist to visit him in the secret People's Prison.

Are you willing, Ambassador, to give an interview to the international Press?

I have no objection.

Let's talk a little about your life in prison, how do you spend your time here?

Well, since my abduction I have felt suspended in time and space. I haven't the slightest idea of the hour, nor the day, nor anything. I wake up, eat, read, sleep again – follow a sort of routine which has become automatic. For instance, I don't know if I'm having breakfast or if I'm having lunch.

What's the food like?

Fairly good – I enjoy it.

Do you get meat?

Sometimes I eat a lot of meat, but lately I've been eating more starchy foods. Probably the reason is that I've lost weight, and now they're making me put it on again.

Have you received any medical attention?

Yes, I'm under medical care. A doctor has visited me two or three times already.

Do you have any exercise?

To a certain extent – I'm following a series of Canadian exercises which make you use up energy equivalent to what you would normally use in an average day.

Do you find it hot here?

Sometimes. But we have a few electric fans – you can hear them – which makes it bearable.

What do you read? Have you asked for any particular books?

Yes, they've been very helpful about reading matter. I like things you can read and reread. I've had *Don Quixote* and *War and Peace*. They brought me the complete works in English of an author I shall reread with much pleasure – Oscar Wilde – and many other books. I'm now reading *Cien Años de Soledad* – a tremendous novel. [' One Hundred Years of Solitude,' by Gabriel Garcia Marquez, a Colombian novelist.]

You were one of the youngest British Ambassadors in Latin America. Your first post as Ambassador was in Honduras, wasn't it?

Yes. But even before that, I was very involved with Latin America.

You were also adviser on Latin American affairs to the British delegation to the United Nations?

Yes.

What do you think are the basic problems of Latin America and what are the possible solutions?

I don't think this is the moment to make profound statements about that, but I suppose the basic need of the continent is to use its wealth in the most practical, intelligent and equitable way.

How long have you been in Uruguay?

Two years.

So you have been able to form an opinion. How do you see Latin America's general problems of which we have been speaking, in terms of Uruguay?

It should become a very privileged country on this continent. It is really one of the few countries in the world where there is land for everyone, and where there is the possibility of feeding all the inhabitants.

Why do you think Uruguay has not realized this possibility? What is holding up this development?

I am sorry – this conversation is extremely interesting, but if I answered that question I would be taking a political stand, which my position as British Ambassador to Uruguay does not allow me to take. I officially represent my country in Uruguay and prefer to keep within the limits of my post. I think you understand that.

Of course, and my question was not intended to compromise you. I was simply trying to make a concrete application of what you just said ... Could you tell me how your abduction took place, how it was carried out, and, above all, how you felt about it?

Well, it was. . . . I'm not saying that the Tupamaros are a blind force, certainly not, but on being kidnapped I felt as if I had been hit by one of those blind forces of nature, like a flash of lightning: in a matter of seconds my whole life was transformed. What is very odd is that I took it all with perfect calmness. I immediately thought certain things out – what would be the effect on my wife, what would happen to me, and I said to myself: well, I must take a philosophical view. It wasn't pleasant, I have to admit that – there was a lot of confusion, but that's all over, thank God.

How was the kidnapping carried out?

We were approaching my office, which is in a part of Montevideo which I thought was absolutely safe against this type of action because never in my life have I managed to travel through those streets without there being half a dozen normal traffic jams. But

they managed it. My car was bumped into by a lorry. My chauffeur said 'What's happening?' Some young men jumped from the lorry with what they called 'fierros' [slang for guns] and they got into the car, pushed out the driver, and a Tupamaro took his place. The street was empty – I don't know if the Tupamaros had blocked the side streets with cars – but we went off at a tremendous speed, making a devil of a noise and with a broken mudguard.

Did you discuss the possibility of being kidnapped with other diplomats?

We talked a lot about these matters. I don't believe there was anyone who hadn't considered the possibility of being kidnapped by the Tupamaros. Up till then they had not taken any ambassadors, but it was pretty clear that somebody had to be the first one. We all expected to be the first. Well, that's the way it goes: it happened to me.

I would like to know what you think about the motives of your kidnappers?

It's very difficult for me to answer. I've been without any information ever since my kidnapping. I don't know what's happened. I don't know what the National Liberation Movement has requested or what has been the reaction of either the Uruguayan Government or my own Government. For that reason, any statement on my part would be mere speculation.

What do you expect from your Government?

That it's going to do all it can to help me get out of this situation.

And from the Uruguayan Government? Remember that President Pacheco Areco, in previous cases, has said that he will not deal with the Tupamaros.

Yes, but as I said, I don't know how the Uruguayan Government may have reacted already.

Perhaps another way of getting out would be for the police to find this hiding place?

I honestly don't know if it would really be a way of getting out. . . .

Meanwhile, what is your relationship with your captors?

We try to live together peacefully which at least changes what could be a hell into a kind of purgatory. We understand each other quite well.

How do you understand each other?

As I said, it's a very acceptable relationship and, in my judgement, very normal. They are in the same situation, with certain shades of difference, so we have to organize ourselves to accept a *modus vivendi* among ourselves. If we don't, life would be impossible and there would be no possibility of sharing a joke once in a while, or of listening together to a bit of music.

Do you remember a typical incident?

Oh yes. I remember the first time they served me a good cup of tea and I started to sing – we have a song in England – 'A Nice Cup of Tea in the Morning.'

Please sing it Ambassador. . . .

Oh, I don't know if. . . .

Please.

'I like a nice cup of tea in the morning, I like a nice cup of tea for my tea. And when I get to bed there's a lot to be said for a nice cup of tea. My voice is not very good, but I remember that when I sang it that day I did it with great satisfaction: it *was* a good cup of tea. It was the first time I managed to laugh and that broke the ice.

I can see you like music a lot. Do you listen to music?

Yes, I've listened to 'El Sabalero' and to Daniel Viglietti. Finally, one day, they brought me Beethoven and Brahms.

From what you tell me, it's not a very usual relationship between a prisoner and his jailers.

It happens that I'm dealing with intelligent people who understand my situation and who try, as much as they can, to see that I don't have a bad time.

You've never been subjected to

abuse or hostility at any moment?
Oh no, absolutely not. Never.

What do you talk about with your guards?

We talk about music, for example, and philosophy and lots about sport.

Perhaps the fact that you find your-self kidnapped has made you change some of your opinions.

In my opinion the kidnappings won't last long. I think they are a fashion like the mini-skirt or maxi-skirt.

Ambassador, aren't you giving political opinions now? For the Tupamaros, kidnappings are a method of revolutionary struggle and you are comparing them with the mini-skirt. I propose fair play. If you wish to give political opinions about the kidnappings, that's fine, but then I must ask you to answer my political questions. It would be logical to assume that you are trying to find the reason for your kidnapping. What conclusions have you come to?

Well, there could be many reasons. The problem is to what extent my analysis is a subjective one. For example, I realize that the Tupamaros, from what I can see, are not sadists and don't want to harm me, but neither do I have the impression that they are sentimental. . . . They may be looking at me with a completely clinical eye. I have the impression

that I'm a kind of experience for the Tupamaros: the first ambassador they've been able to observe. It's difficult for me to make definite judgements at this stage, but I've already been able to reach certain conclusions about the type of mentality of a young Tupamaro which I hadn't been able to do before.

What are those conclusions?

For example, they are hard working, very serious, have great dynamism, are completely dedicated. But I belong to another generation and had a different education and I would like to see them being more open-minded. Perhaps this is an attitude typical of young people and, in five or ten years, they may develop their thinking.

Excuse me, but I didn't completely understand the last part of your statement.

What I mean to say is that a Tupamaro is a Tupamaro. He commits himself fully to his ideal. And I ask myself whether or not this is only youthful enthusiasm. I think that a Tupamaro who is 20 years old is not interested in reading things that may contradict his beliefs.

On what do you base that statement?

It's not a statement. I'm trying to guess. . . .

Don't you think that it is a matter

of an organization which has defined a political line after analysing the reality of the situation? Such a line could be considered objective – for it is the result of a confrontation of opinions.

Perhaps I could answer you, but I'm beginning to feel a bit tired. I think that what you've said deserves analysis.

I don't want you to get tired. If you prefer, we can stop for a while or talk about something else. For example, what are the differences between the opinion you had of the Tupamaros before you were kidnapped and the one you have now?

I have found them much more human than I expected.

I would like to return to something you said before: that your guards are also going through a form of detention.

I've thought about this, and I've realized that these young people are suffering painful tensions similar to mine. At certain moments I've had the impression that they have had to control themselves with great effort.

My question was directed at precisely that. There is a difference between the tension that they endure voluntarily and the one you have to endure by force. How do you explain this?

Well, they have a cause. And when people dedicate themselves to a cause, they accept it with all the risks involved – they volunteer for it.

How do you value that?

As a very honourable, ethical attitude of carrying out to the end their sincere convictions. Oh, there's something else that must be added about their intentions. This is of great importance, because if they did what they did out of a desire for financial gain or for personal ambition, then it would be ignoble.

Have you found in them any traces of such a motive?

No. I see them as sincere idealists.

What do you think they're after? What sort of ideals do they have?

They're revolutionary. And, of course, it's a point that I lament because I believe in evolution. They are all dedicated and that is why they speak and act in such a serious fashion.

Assuming that that is also their point of view, can you justify your abduction in terms of the service it will render to the Tupamaros and their cause?

Right from the start I thought they committed a tactical error with my abduction. I don't see what they can get out of it. And I've thought about this a lot. I could be wrong because I am so personally involved in the matter.

APPENDIX 2

Maruja Echegoyen Interview
(*Interviewer's questions in italic*)

On March 27, after six weeks of indirect negotiations I arrived at the 'people's jail' with a hood over my head. They led me into a narrow place and announced: 'You can begin your interview now. Ambassador Jackson is in front of you.'

I asked permission to take off my hood; they grudgingly granted my request.

Seated in front of me on a bunk in cell No. 10 was Ambassador Jackson in very good shape. He was freshly shaven, cordial and expectant, dressed in a pink shirt and shorts – looking exactly the same as when I met him a year ago in London. I explained to him that a faithful version of the interview would be distributed to the serious press.

But I haven't structured the interview Ambassador. I wasn't sure if I would see you. Everything was done in such an indirect way that I wasn't sure if I was victim of a Uruguayan joke. . . .

No, it's no joke (laughing).

I felt it was extremely important that you identify yourself, in general terms. And that I know that the interview is being used for serious purposes. Within that framework, yes, I accept the interview with great pleasure.

A few questions gave us the biographical data: He was born in the northern, industrial city of Bolton in England.

He read modern languages: French, German, Italian and Spanish at Cambridge University and he also studied economics, history, etc. to pass his exams for the diplomatic service.

He is married and has a 27-year-old son.

He comes from Anglican and Catholic parentage, but his mother's religion finally prevailed. He's now a practising Catholic.

But he did not have any strong religious or political leaning: 'I must be by nature the almost ideal British officer: I've always been a man of the centre, without strong political orientation.'

Ambassador, I'm going to ask you a touchy question, perhaps a bit crazy. It's been said that you didn't take any precautions. Deep down, did you want to be kidnapped?

No, no, no. That's crazy. I took a lot of reasonable precautions.

But I didn't go around as if I were in a state of war. One has certain restrictions to arrive at one's office and one's home: I took all the necessary precautions. This is not the moment to go into details, but my people know that perfectly. And psychologically I'm not such a complicated man!

The phenomenon of the secretly wished accident is very well known. I'm not saying you planned it, but actually . . . for example, weren't you bored with your career? Didn't you want something different and unusual to happen to you?

It's almost worth going through this extremely disagreeable experience, this horror, to listen to such complicated explanations. No, I would have been very happy to continue my life as it was. . . . I didn't have any intention of writing the definitive book about revolutionary urban guerrillas. Nothing of the sort (he laughs).

If I could turn the clock back to last Jan. 8 and continue my way to my office, I would do it with the greatest pleasure, thank you very much, Madam.

And the other interpretation . . . the totally fantastic one? I am asking you out of, let us say, curiosity. Let's suppose that you are one of the top British secret agents and that you managed to get

yourself kidnapped to learn from the inside the mentality of this unknown people, their methods and some way to uncover them. Is it another crazy idea?

James Bond has been so successful that people are likely to believe anything. One must have a very lazy mind to spend time thinking such complicated explanations. They sooner do that than work.

No, I am strictly an English diplomat, trained in the traditional system and my main interest lies in the field of trade and things of that type. So none of those James Bond-type speculations!

Would you like to talk about how you spend your time? Have you always been kept in this small place?

We have an agreement between us here. I consider myself as what I am: the ambassador from Great Britain, still accredited in Uruguay. That is why I don't want to talk about certain things where we have completely opposite points of view.

For example, my position as a kidnapped person, as a victim. We've agreed to live together . . . so that this will be only a purgatory and not a hell. Our living together means that I've given my word of honour not to speak of certain things in detail.

I could answer your question. Yes, I've been in another place, but I can't go into details without violating my word of honour.

What I'm simply interested in is how you live. What do they feed you, for example?

I have a healthy, simple very well-balanced diet . . . more or less what I normally eat in my home: a lot of meat and salad. Perhaps I eat a bit more potatoes and rice, and one becomes – like any prisoner – a bit dependent on food, like the lion in its cage. I begin to pace around saying: 'I'm ready for the next meal.' But I cannot say that I've ever been hungry. I eat well. . . .

I read that you liked apples so I brought you some, not very good but the best I could find today. . . .

Ah, God bless you.

I also brought you two books. A detective novel and another one of short stories, both in English. I didn't know you were Catholic. I have some very good revolutionary Catholic literature. It might have interested you. Or not?

But you know that I know nothing of what is going on in the world. I'm completely without any news of the outside world!

Don't you read newspapers?

No. I don't know what day it is, or what hour . . . I don't know whether a nuclear bomb has exploded . . . I'm a bit isolated, so I appreciate your comment a great deal.

I've read in the accounts of prisoners that one of the problems is how to structure time so as not to get bored or desperate. What do you do? Do you read, play cards?

One must get personally organized. God has given me a very active and positive type of mind and imagination. I plan my day: I spend a lot of time thinking. I try to imagine what goes on in the world. I don't dwell too much on my own case, otherwise I would go crazy.

I work a few hours a day and lead a very active spiritual life. I often interrupt my activities during the day to do physical exercises. Given the limitations of the surroundings I do the Canadian exercises, 5BX. I've galloped and trotted kilometres and kilometres during the 100 days of jail.

What are you reading for example?

I was lucky. In the place I was in before there was an old edition of Tolstoy's *Anna Karenina*. I read it again – not for Anna Karenina – she is a very foolish woman – but for another character I loved. Then I got hold of *War and Peace* which I've read several times during my life.

I've also read *Don Quijote* twice. Of course, I also read the Bible. Fortunately the Tupamaros have been very considerate in this respect. They realized that I needed the Bible and they did not delay in getting it in both English and Spanish.

I imagine that due to your education you become interested in the history and thinking of the countries where you are sent. Have you had a chance to talk about this with the people around you or do you only talk about trivial matters?

There's a basic problem here. One must not forget that I'm in solitary confinement. These young people are my guards. We say a few things through the bars but they are not my cellmates. We don't have a social relationship.

I can ask them questions that are not of an overly essential nature; we don't hold any profound conversations. No, frankly, I'm a prisoner – and there should be no misunderstanding about this – a very lonely one. You spoke about 100 years of solitude (in discussing a Latin American book). Well, I don't know how many days have passed, but I imagine that they are around 100 days and I'm feeling them. . . .

I understand you . . . but I supposed that due to your isolation and solitude – and out of human curiosity – you would want to learn.

You are now asking me a question as an ambassador and I will answer only as an ambassador. I'm not willing to answer such a question as an individual. And as an ambassador I only answer to Her Majesty's government.

I can't ask this question of Ambassador Jackson, but what I'm interested in is Mr. Jackson. Can't I ask you as a human being what you think of the problem? Are you giving an entirely free answer? Or are you afraid that what you will answer may be misinterpreted or ill-used?

Oh, I'm not at all afraid. It's always the same problem, especially with my journalist friends. How many times have they told me: 'Now please answer as an individual, not as an ambassador.' But it's impossible. In such circumstances one is always an ambassador. Perhaps someday I will answer you personally, but I can't at the moment.

But even as an ambassador you could give a general opinion about basic things. . . . The American revolution stated, for example, that governments derive their power from the consent of the people. If the government doesn't use its power legitimately, the people have the right to overthrow it. . . . Don't you accept the right to revolution even within that context?

This is a very curious place to receive such an intellectual confrontation. These are things that would be difficult to answer even around a table. I would be very pleased, Madam, to answer you but I can't.

It seems a bit scholastic to launch suddenly into the theory of revolution and such profound things as the rights of man in such a tense situation. I prefer to leave it for another occasion. Perhaps someday, I hope in my house in London, we can stretch our legs and speak profoundly about such matters.

I imagine that you've become somewhat interested in the history of the Uruguayan people, their historical figures, and their evolution. Without going into details, could you tell us which Uruguayan historical figure you like the best and why?

I shall be very pleased! I've known Uruguay indirectly for nearly 30 years. I've books in my house for example, about Artigas. (José Gervasio Artigas led Uruguay to short-lived independence in 1814 during the Latin American wars of liberation against Spain. It wasn't until 1828 that Uruguay won final independence after being occupied by Brazil.)

I know the Latin American independence heroes very well, and Artigas, is one of the most 'simpático' – especially because in a way he failed.

He failed although there was tremendous human success in his failure. He left a legend and a state. British participation in all of this is particularly interesting for me.

I was surprised, if I may say so – and this is to answer your previous question – that a group of Uruguayans would kidnap an Englishman. I never believed it just because of that historical link with British diplomacy. But of course, I was wrong.

You speak of Artigas as a figure of the past. Don't you believe that his ideals and hopes are still relevant in Uruguay?

Yes and how! And if not, look at the members of this organization, the Tupamaros. They are extremely influenced by the memory and ideas of Artigas. They speak a great deal about him and it's obvious that they have a great deal of respect for Artigas, not only as a military man but as a statesman.

Yes, Artigas is a very relevant figure in this country.

I believe that a serious and dedicated study of Artigas and his ideals would be a very healthy thing for any Uruguayan and for the country to undertake.

I seem to detect in what you said just now – that the Uruguayans would not kidnap an Englishman – some wounded sense of 'fair-play'. Assuming that what they wanted was to kidnap an Englishman, don't you see anything in British history that would make the Uruguayans of today – who read history with more critical eyes – react with anti-English feelings?

I'm surprised if that's the way they look at things. It's an extremely superficial analysis. The fact that Her Majesty's government in certain things follows the same world policy as that of other allied countries does not mean that we have totally adapted ourselves to them. There is no justification to say that we follow the United States in its Latin American policies, like a blind man. If that's the way we're judged, then they've studied the facts very badly.

But, you can understand the attitude of the young people who believe that capitalism has brought tremendous suffering to Latin America and continues to maintain the Latin American countries in a form of economic slavery. So, any great ally of the United States would seem to be, for these young people, an enemy of their own cause.

If the young people are going about inventing honorary enemies what can we do? But we don't consider ourselves the enemy of any country or of any Latin American generation. If they invent reasons, if they look for

hatred where there is none . . . But that's natural in youth. I've been young myself.

Forty years ago we talked about these very same things at the University of Cambridge. One shouldn't believe everything one believes when one is 20 years old. With five or 10 more years of study, they would see that not everybody is their enemy, that they have many friends all over the world, including us.

I wasn't speaking of subjective things. Undoubtedly, there are young people who are superficial and badly informed . . . I was speaking of economic and political realities – of the exploitation of Latin America by capitalism, of the extraction of our wealth and primary products, of the maintenance of dictatorial governments favourable to the United States, of the overthrowing of the liberal ones, things you don't have to be a Marxist or a Communist – which I am not – to see clearly because they are historic realities. Don't you think that the fact that England is so allied to the United States in the exploitation of Latin America – although you, your government and the people around you may be personally innocent – don't you think that this produces a historically justified reaction?

It would seem so. As far as all this concerns me, my country is giving much material aid to Uruguay, with quite broad credits and quite low interest rates. I am speaking of completely normal commercial affairs. I don't see that one can honestly say that this country is totally exploited and taken advantage of that way and with a type of collaboration on our part. I think that there is an obsession in all this.

I agree: Latin America must struggle to make good sales of its basic products in the world, but Latin American industry already exists. In my opinion, Latin America is struggling not too badly. It is not a struggle that has completely failed.

And the fact that these industries – especially in Argentina and Brazil, in other countries as well, are in the hands of foreign capital, do you think this is an indication that the continent is becoming liberated? Isn't there a concealed, insidious legally perfect and patriotically criminal way of using the goods of one country for the benefit of the foreign investor?

I am very interested in your denial . . . because you know sometimes non-existent declarations are used for not very honest purposes.

I have never made, nor would I ever make, a declaration concerning the internal affairs of a country because that would be the crudest interference that a diplomat could make. I will never do that and I have never done it.

Yes, I expected that from a British diplomat. Now, if you would like to answer this question, and since you told me you were a Catholic (I am one too and I am very interested in the development of the Catholic church in Latin America) . . . very serious studies are being made on the theology of revolution and the liberation of Latin America, etc. Have you followed some movements, for example, the Third World priests in Argentina, the Golconda group in Colombia, the Young Church in Chile, Uruguayan theology?

Yes I've followed what is happening in Uruguay pretty closely. On Sundays, after mass, I buy *Ciudad Nueva*. I know many people of that young group. I am in . . . auditive contact with them. I'm interested in the sermons that speak of that type of thing. Extremely interested. Whenever a book that deals with that theme is sold at the church door, I always buy it. The subject impassions me.

Do you know magazines such as 'Vispera' or 'Notebooks for Dialogue'?

I've seen them at times, but I don't subscribe to them. I have to read so many things! But I'm familiar with almost all those magazines. I more or less understand the situation here, yes.

What do you think of Camillo Torres, the Colombian priest, the guerrilla who was murdered?
Well . . . I would prefer . . . not to answer. Because I have . . . there are attitudes and points of view that are very . . . very personal. What do you think, for example, of a finger, a hand, that is consecrated? A consecrated finger – does it have the right to pull the trigger? And if it has pulled the trigger should an honest Catholic accept the body of his God from the same hand?

Don't you understand that there could be a historical situation in which a priest, or a convinced Catholic realizes that the only way to live the 'love each other' way is to stop, by force, all killing and torturing . . . of others?
I understand your question very well, but . . . in spite of the fact that we are talking under such unique, rare and fascinating circumstances, I am still the British Ambassador.

And just as people have quoted me as saying something that could be called an interference, if I answered your question now, I would fall in the same trap. A diplomat does not have the right to answer such questions. If I say: 'Yes, I am in agreement – one has such a right,' then the president to

whom I am accredited would have the right to be angry, and the people with him.

It would be as if I had made a criticism of the president himself. Our situation today is very, very complicated. We cannot say things that would criticize, or be construed as criticism, of the government. In this case, I withdraw and say: 'No comment'.

I simply ask you – since you referred to the consecrated finger that pulls the trigger – I asked you for your theological definition of the uses of violence that could be employed by a Christian acting temporally to eliminate injustice . . . I also asked you for your opinion of Catholic theologians.
But look . . . it's like a war. Just as soon as you get on to theology, well . . . a Christian has the right to be a pacifist or he can justify going off to war. The existence of a 'just war' has been justified many times – or tried to be justified. Take the last war. No doubt about it, we all knew what our friend Hitler was.

Your question is on the same level: Is there a justifiable civil war, as there are justifiable international wars? Unfortunately I cannot answer the question right now because my answer under the present circumstances will correspond to a comment on topical matters, which I am not in a position to do.

Would you like me to take some special message to your family in London?

Well ... that's very kind of you, but there are so many things to say. No, I want to see them. I don't know how much longer I shall continue this way. I'm very patient. I try to be firm. What worries me is my poor wife. That is, it is she who ... At least I know how I spent my day. I know how I wake up. As the Psalms say: 'I lay me down and sleep and the Lord watches over me.' But with her ... I don't know how she is ... That's my problem. I don't know how she spends her days.

If she is a good Catholic, as you say she is, she probably has the same fortitude and the same hope you have. ...

Yes, I know ... but there are other matters, such as health ...

and another thing worries me: The only aspect of a visit which has enchanted me and of an interview which has given me great pleasure ... is this business of a 'death wish' ... of a so-called secret desire of mine ... and that very complicated interpretation.

It has left me ... a little ... I won't say hurt, but ...

Please don't worry about that. I am not repeating things that were said publicly. Your person inspires great sympathy. ...

Especially since my conscience is so clean ... I did my utmost, given the circumstances, and I have no intention to justify myself. I am not before a court, I am not accused of anything. I am an innocent prisoner, in every aspect. So, I put all these things from my mind, until I return to a normal life and to my family.

My government will understand.